How Not to Raise a Perfect Child

Libby Purves was a late starter, having her first baby at thirty-two. However, this gave her time to accumulate some useful experience, working as a barmaid, broadcaster, travelling reporter and as the editor – for six exciting months – of the society magazine *Tatler*. This career gave her a valuable grounding in the motherly arts of pacifying unreasonable individuals, managing without sleep, and being able to talk her way out of trouble. In 1986, with children aged two and three, she was so exasperated by the perfectionist tone of other child-care books that she wrote the much-loved *How Not to Be a Perfect Mother*. In 1988 she and her husband, Paul Heiney, set out to sail 1700 miles round Britain in their small boat with children of three and five. She published the story in *One Summer's Grace* (1990). Her most recent book (1994) is *How Not to Be a Perfect Family*.

She lives in Suffolk with her husband and children (now aged nine and eleven) on a small farm, travels to London once a week to present the Radio 4 programme 'Midweek', and writes for *The Times* and other newspapers and magazines.

NOT

How/to Raise a Perfect Child

The canny parent's guide to childhood

Libby Purves

Drawings by Viv Quillin

■ HarperCollins*Publishers*

HarperCollins*Publishers*
77–85 Fulham Palace Road,
Hammersmith, London W6 8JB

This paperback edition 1994
1 3 5 7 9 8 6 4 2

Previously published in paperback by Fontana 1991
Reprinted twice

ISBN 0 00 637598 7

Set in Palatino

Printed in Great Britain by
HarperCollinsManufacturing Glasgow

To all primary school teachers everywhere

Your children are not your children
They are the sons and daughters of
Life's longing for itself.
They come through you but not from you
And though they are with you, yet they belong not to you.
You may give them your love but not your thoughts,
For they have their own thoughts.
You may house their bodies but not their souls,
For their souls dwell in the house of tomorrow which you cannot
    visit, not even in your dreams.
You may strive to be like them, but seek not to make them like you.
For life goes not backward nor tarries with yesterday.

KAHLIL GIBRAN,
'The Prophet', 1923

Contents

Acknowledgements   xi
Introduction   1

1 Farewell, Fat Legs: Why three is different   4
2 First Friends: Other people's children   11
3 Mum-upmanship: Other children's parents   18
4 The Dawn of Discipline: Sense, slaps and self-defence   25
5 Television: Is there a cure?   35
6 Fair's Fair: Quibbling siblings   39
7 Coaching Days: Classes, courses, push and shove   45
8 Widening the Circle: Bachelors and babysitters   50
9 Money Talks: But what does it say?   59
10 Hard Wearing: Cracking the dress code   66
11 Heavy Petting: Terrible gerbils and gangland goldfish   71
12 Toys: Junk and joyfulness   78
13 The Good Granny Guide   89
14 Faith, Fears, and Legends   94
15 Below the Belt: And bum to you, too   104
16 Party Politics: Taking the cake   110
17 And so to School: What, neurotic? Me?   116
18 Talking Proper: Murder most vowel   128
19 Whoopee: Treats and trips   135
20 On the Mend: Hospitals and hacking coughs   146
21 On the Run: Mummy does a bunk   157
22 Is That All There Is? The last baby   163
23 Envoi: More to them than meets the eye   168

Index   171

Acknowledgements

Firstly great thanks are due to my husband Paul, to our children, and to my friends, and my friends' children, who have wittingly and unwittingly contributed to this book. Nor would it have been written without the steadfast – not to say importunate – insistence of certain periodical editors over the past five years that, despite my protests to the contrary, I ought to think, research, and write about children. In this context I thank Jackie Highe, Daphne Metland, Tony Bradman and Sandra Lane of *Parents* magazine in particular.

The attitudes and insights of countless other people have been borrowed, magpie-fashion, over the same period: particular thanks for such wisdoms to the staff of Coldfair Green School, to Christina Hardyment, to Janet Bellis, Caroline Stevens, Belinda Devenish, Robin Skynner, Martin Herbert, and – as usual – my mother.

Introduction

Never apologize, never explain. When I finished *How Not to be a Perfect Mother* I said grandly that this was the end. From conception to the fourth birthday party, there was some excuse for reading – or writing – baby books. It seemed to me that in the early stages it is reasonable to generalize; although a baby is an individual, in early life the common qualities far outweigh the differences. *All* six-month-old babies grab the spoon when you try to feed them; *all* new walkers pull things off tables on to their heads; and the particular qualities of a two-year-old (not unlike a suitcaseful of gelignite on a cake-walk) are pretty universal too. But after four years, I wrote, 'You may have acquired a tough gunslinger or a dainty Victorian miss (of either sex); an intellectual or an athlete or a socialite. They stand apart from one another, small but separate, each on a private platform of heredity and chance and conditioning. So a mature three seemed a good age at which to stop.'

And, I added loudly to my friends, there would in future be no question of my writing another book about looking after children. If you hadn't got the hang of your own child by four years old you must be past helping. So no more advice from me: I had served my time as a baby-pundit, and would get back to writing about other things. I was quite glad,

1

really: never again would I have to decide whether to refer to a child as 'he' (old-fashioned), 'she' (trendy) or 'it' (offensive), or whether to overburden every other sentence with such lumbering hybrids as 'he/she'. I never did solve that one, and never will.

But I was wrong. I eat my words. My own children grew older, but as the memories of nappies and night-alarms began to fail, instead of relaxing into a new, rational phase of family life I found myself still at sea. I was still working to make sense of it all, and above all still animatedly comparing notes with my mother friends of all ages, and also with total strangers in supermarket queues. The children's maturity and self-sufficiency had made some things infinitely easier: far less time was used up in physical service to the children, and a certain rationality crept in as toddlerhood receded. After four, one can make deals like 'Give me ten minutes peace with the paper and *then* we'll start the Meccano roundabout.' When a four-year-old wants a yoghurt, one can point at the fridge and say 'All right, go and choose', without pausing in one's energetic attempts to unblock the kitchen drain. By five, one can have good grounds for believing that the child will remember to shut the fridge door. At six, he will be shutting it extra fast because school and 'green' television programmes have made him very concerned about not wasting electricity. It is definitely easier, in some ways.

But the goal posts had been moved, and new issues came up which had never much troubled the baby years: nightmares, swearing, school, sleepovers, parties, television, mumps, smacking, the Tooth Fairy, that sort of thing. They combine into endless new pictures: many a happy, fascinated hour has been spent chewing the fat with my friends on such issues as what to do if your child has nightmares about the Tooth Fairy, or swears at school, or gives everyone else mumps at his party. One day I realized that everything had changed, yet nothing had. Instead of mashing up bananas with a baby on one arm while singing 'Nellie the Elephant' to a toddler, I was simultaneously building an eggbox model of a spaceship while booking swimming lessons on the telephone and trying to explain why aeroplanes fly. And I decided that perhaps there was a sequel to write, after all.

It is not much like the first book, simply because those goal posts have moved. By this stage of parenthood, there is less point in offering ten quick ways to distract a baby, or a pageful of other people's brilliant solutions to the potty problem. There is no need to pass on humble tips about putting masking tape in hotel baths to stop a toddler slipping (frankly, by five years old my children were a lot more nimble and less likely to fall over than I was). If you think about it, it would be positively insulting to write a three-to-eight book in the same tone as a baby book: small children are a massive management problem, within which a relationship is growing. With bigger children, the relationship is in the foreground and although there is still a place for low cunning on the mother's part, it has to be a lot better disguised. Why else do four- and five-year-olds so suddenly, and disconcertingly, outgrow their fondness for certain very mumsy babysitters and nannies? They are changing. A parent's job is to change with them. That is what the book is about.

Above all, perhaps, it is another swipe at the idea of perfection in family life. Whereas in the first couple of years the pressure is on to be a Perfect Mother, a modern Madonna with her armoury of fluoride drops and educational flashcards and endless self-sacrificing patience, as the child grows up the emphasis changes. Suddenly it is *the child* who is expected to be a perfect, glossy specimen: well-balanced, well-behaved, artistic, scientific and physically adept. Instead of being impressed with guilt about your own inadequacy and inefficiency as a mother, you are forever being pricked into unease by subliminal suggestions that your child is not quite up to scratch: not passing the tests, learning the cello, making the team. Fight it. There is no such thing as an ideal child, any more than there is a perfect parent.

Never mind, by the way, if that parent happens to be a mother, father, or both. As far as I am concerned, 'mother' is a job description, not a definition of sex.

1. Farewell Fat Legs: Why three is different

A curious change comes over children at three to four years old. It is not as obvious as the earlier changes, like standing upright or speaking or giving up nappies; and there is not as much written about it. But it happens, often quite suddenly, and it needs responding to. If you go on treating a big child the same way as you dealt with a toddler, you will waste as much effort and cause as much aggravation as if you forced nappies on to a schoolchild or tried to carry a teenager everywhere in a backpack. Yet you can miss the changes at first: parenthood is tiring and confusing. Its vision is misted by love and anxiety and one's own childhood memories, good or bad; not to mention other people's doctrinaire theories splashed all over the newspapers and the baby books. You can miss changes that are happening right in front of your eyes, though many of them are things which, taken the right way, would actually make everyone's life a lot easier. You can find you are wasting half an hour chivvying your baby off to bed while you miss the six o'clock television news – when , in fact, what you have there is no baby, but a young child of rising six, who would be quite interested to watch the news with you and have a solemn discussion about *perestroika* before going off to bed at about the same time he would have anyway.

The border between toddlerhood and childhood is a real one. I have often thought that there must be a magical protective quality in fat legs; a baby or toddler has a cheerful, roundish, uncompromising sort of shape. Solid chubby legs seem to go well with an opinionated and highly practical outlook on life. A toddler's jokes are uproarious, his wishes imperious, his temper uncontrollable and his actions – as far as he is concerned – totally without consequences. Someone will mop it up. Someone will mend it. We shall buy anuzzer one, Mummy, at the shops. There is no problem so pressing that a hug and a warm drink can't solve it.

Then the child changes shape: everything grows lengthways and slims down. Fat legs turn into long spindly ones, the protruding tummy develops graceful hollows, and suddenly your ex-baby has begun to turn large, worried, wondering eyes on the rest of the universe. Why is it raining? Will the mouse never come alive again if Tibby bites it dead? Will I go to prison if I say a rude word to a policeman?

The difference came home to me when my own two children were on either side of it. An item came up on 'Blue Peter' about the hole in the ozone layer. The elder child took days to calm down from the swirling black fears it stirred up: a hole in the sky, letting in bad rays and making the sea flood us! There was real horror in his eyes. The three-year-old merely said 'Ahahaaa! We shall all fry up, frizzle, frizzle!' without believing a word of it. At first I thought it was a mere difference in their temperaments: but then I remembered that a year earlier Nicholas had had the same gung-ho, sanguine approach to life, and suspected (correctly as it turns out) that in a year's time Rose too would fall prey to cosmic fears. And a memory came back: decades ago I lay in my bed, aged six, shivering with fear at the thought of the new nuclear power station up the road – Sizewell A. I had found out about radioactivity. So had my little brother, but he was merely thrilled at the idea that he might be radioactive one day. He wanted to glow all over, 'like a gloo017inous watch'.

It is easy to misjudge the borderline: it can happen any time between four and six, and if you are busy, or harassed by younger children, you can miss it. You can also miss it if you have got so good at the physical, reassuring, singing, playing side of mothering that you find it difficult to let go of the tried and tested responses. I found myself going on too long with the cheery, protective, prattling nonsense which keeps a toddler happy, when my child was asking for more concentrated listening and serious talk. 'Mummy,' he said crossly, 'don't make a joke of everything.' But it is a very easy mistake to make: sometimes it helps to go away from your child for a day or two, so that you can come back and look with a rather more detached eye at what is being demanded of you.

You have to: because this is as serious a demand as the baby's cries for milk ever were. Growing up is tough, and this four-year-old stage is almost like a rehearsal for adolescence. That child may seem to be an active, cheerful, destructive bundle of animal spirits, riding a bike and building Lego models, but he is also going through great bewilderments and revelations. He is grasping all sorts of concepts and adult truth which will rock the foundations of his small world: it is like discovering a new planet, or a new scientific law, or a new religion every week.

Take death, for instance: tell a two-year-old that Grandad has gone to heaven, and that is that. A couple of years later the same event strikes home with a new and awful significance. Even if you use the idea of heaven to soften the blow, you have to admit that people (and pet rabbits) don't come back from death, not ever. This so appalled my children, each in turn, that for a while even the bang-bang-you're-dead games were modified. 'I'll shoot yer dead', they would say, 'but not dead to heaven, just bang dead.'

Smaller matters cause upsets too. For months we were driven crazy by the droning repetition of 'I want one of my own.' We could no longer go, as we had six months earlier, to a steam fair or a railway museum and share the uncomplicated joys of looking at the machines. Our daughter, still two, happily waved goodbye at the end of a day's treat; her anxious elder brother nagged all the way home for a steam locomotive 'of my own', a private cinema, or a real traction engine to keep in his bedroom. He sometimes got quite aggressive about it. It would have been easy to assume that we had bred a spoilt and materialistic monster, but we held our irritation in check for most of the time. We had a theory, and I believe it is true, that he was actually expressing not greed, but a sort of shock and fear at having realized the temporariness of things. He had suddenly realized that treats and visits come to an end, earth's comforts flee and pleasures pass away. Since then I have heard of children who cry bitterly before their birthdays, because they are thinking how sad it will be when the day ends. You can't do much to help, but you can try to understand.

The baby lived blithely for the moment, but the child bears a burden of unfulfilled and delayed longings. Time is long, the world is wide: on a good day the four-year-old is delighted with the idea. Stories about when Mummy was little, or countries far away, or what you can do when you are grown up, all get a raptly attentive audience. On a bad day, the child only wants the world to be small and cosy again. So suddenly he – or she – will cling. All parents seem to get patches when their child wants to stay at home, and refuses point-blank to go to the playgroup where he has been perfectly happy for a year. He prefers the boredom of sitting on the floor beside a furiously busy and grumpy Mummy. He doesn't want to do big, brave grown-up things or see his friends or have new books read or watch the Punch and Judy. He wants to sit on a knee and have the ten thousandth reading of *Polly Pig and the Bee* (my least favourite children's book of all time). All the childcare books stress the importance of 'socialization', but I have yet to meet a parent who didn't admit that between three and eight there were occasional unaccountable periods – days, weeks, or months long – when their child appeared to hate all other children and refuse outings.

It can be difficult, frustrating, boring and embarrassing for the parents: it makes it easier if you consider that fear of the outside world is a perfectly understandable part of discovering it. When my children were tiny and played on the beach on their chubby legs, I often thought sentimentally of Isaac Newton's words at the end of his life: 'To myself I seem to have been only a child playing on the seashore . . . whilst the great ocean of truth lay undiscovered before me.' In those days they were indeed looking at each shiny stone, concentrating on what was close and touchable and throwable. It is as they grow older that their eyes become raised in half-troubled wonderment, and they notice the great ocean of undiscovered truth stretching away from their feet. It is no wonder that they sometimes hesitate to confront it.

But time wears on, and children learn fast. By six or seven

they will have worked out, with your help, a basic philosophy on dealing with the vastness and risk of life. They become increasingly keen on action rather than fantasy: instead of demanding real traction engines of their own, they go outside with a heap of junk and convince themselves they are building one. Instead of merely quailing with horror at the realization that children in the Third World are starving, they start collecting stamps and drink-cans for 'Blue Peter' or a school fund-raising appeal. They love the idea of laws and rules: they read out speed limits to you in the car, and when the new British law came in that children must wear seat-belts, it was the children who righteously did them up, squeaking furiously if their parents drove off before they were clipped in.

So these are the thinking years, the years when you pass on your personal philosophy to your child. Your social, spiritual and emotional values are on their way to the next generation. This is a distinctly alarming prospect. Most of us manage to scramble through young adulthood without being aware of having a personal philosophy at all. Teenagers think about morality and ethics, and old people consider eternity: but unless you are a fervently committed believer of one kind or another, the years you pass in getting and spending and scrabbling around in the everyday world of work and mortgages do tend to blur the eternal verities. We may know which political party we support and whether or not we approve of adultery, lead-free petrol and private education; but we start to flounder a bit when a questing four-year-old starts coming up with questions about why God lets people die in earthquakes, why Mister Rushdie had to go into hiding, or why Daddy shouts rude things at the Prime Minister on television when everybody knows that the government is demmercratically elected by everybody.

It is actually rather healthy that we do flounder. It indicates that we are trying to find the truth, and willing to share our uncertainties with our children. There is something depressing about people whose beliefs make them sure that they know it all: they seem so often to raise little bigots.

The best parents share a few uncertainties with their children, in a spirit of interested, positive questing. To take a fashionable issue as an example, they don't say 'Wicked people are cutting down the rainforests because they are greedy and bad', but haver about, more or less creatively, trying to explain about poor farmers, international loans, beleaguered governments and ignorance. With a bit of luck, they conclude with something relatively simple like the fact that cutting down rainforests is a bad thing for the planet, and that all people of goodwill must try to help the South Americans, Indonesians, and others not to do it. Such parents may tie themselves into knots occasionally and bring down mockery from others – there are few spectacles so richly comic as a concerned mummy trying to explain her

environmental philosophy in a supermarket queue – but they are doing a more intelligent job than those who say 'Never mind the rainforests, get on with your tea.'

Mind you, there are some impossible questions. It is no fun to be confronted with such questions as 'Tell me the real truth, is there a Father Christmas?' or 'If Daddy loved me, why did he go away?' And there will be moments when the policy of open, questing discussion of big issues will come unstuck. Years ago we had a child of seven or eight to stay whose parents were dynamic and utterly open in their discussion. In one afternoon we heard them talking rationally and helpfully to him about nuclear war, lesbianism, terrorist bombs, child molesters and the death penalty. We were lost in admiration of this open and fearless family. Then at supper Paul and I started telling the assembled company about how we had just got rid of a plague of big rats in our creaking farmhouse larder. The little boy's eyes grew wider and wider, and he went white. It took his mother hours to get him to sleep, and she was pretty cross with us for mentioning something so alarming. The lad had come to terms with a potential nuclear holocaust and any number of bombs, but he drew the line at rats. Even dead rats. Not being his parents, we got it wrong: we weren't close enough to know his terrors.

The point is to stay close. Not smotheringly close – this is the age of the playroom, of vanishing upstairs with friends for hours of private games – but near enough to pick up the signals. Listen when you're being talked to. It is hard, especially hard if you have gone back to work and would prefer nice mindless romps and cuddles of an evening; but listening to young children's preoccupations and talking sense to them is as important as giving them books and cleaning their teeth, and a lot more important than combing their hair or nagging them to eat with the fork the right way up. It counts for more than fashionable violin lessons and expensive educational toys. It is the one corner you can't cut: and coming from a confirmed corner-cutter like myself, that is quite an admission.

2. First Friends: Other people's children

For the first four years, your children have to put up with your friends. For the next fourteen, you are stuck with theirs. Crawling babies will crawl round the room together while their mothers gossip, toddlers will adapt – albeit grudgingly – to the company of whatever peers you plonk down in front of them. But once a healthy child gets to kindergarten age and meets what psychologists call 'a pool of eligibles', the choice is taken from you. 'Gillie is my best friend,' they will say firmly, and however bored you are by Gillie's vapid gossip of a mother, you must smile and make friends and have them to tea. It is only fair. (Actually, you might get to like Gillie's mother: some of the nicest couples I know are those whose children my own have adopted at school or playgroup. But even if you don't, you are stuck with it.)

You daren't impede friendship, of any kind, because the worst dread of all is that your child won't make friends. Suppose he stands alone in the playgroup, alone in the playground? Break, heart! I can think of nothing in routine parenthood which wrings your withers more painfully than the sight of your own child standing sadly on the borderline, or chosen last when the teams are picked. I am a confident enough type, myself, yet I have never given a children's birthday party without a crazy secret dread that nobody would turn up. This results, of course, in my inviting too many and spending half the night filling twenty party bags and willing the jelly to set: and, needless to say, they all come and we run out of chairs. But it is the worst, coldest fear to have for your child: that he or she will grow up without the gift of friendship.

Because, after all, what else is there? There is no point being rich or beautiful or brilliant if you're lonely. And of all human relationships, the most reliable and least painful is real friendship. Even the best marriages are founded largely upon it. Whatever happens to my children in the next seventy years, if I were granted one wish for them I would ask the fairy godmother to guarantee that at the end of each fraught day there would always be a few numbers they can ring, and a welcoming sofa they can sleep on when they're down. Then, and only then, can I reconcile myself to the fact of my own eventual disappearance.

The moment when your own child first thrusts a toy train under another toddler's nose, willing him to take it or look at it, is the beginning of all this. Try to note the moment. It may not last long, since the next stage is, with regrettable frequency, a sudden change of mind and a sharp blow on the head with the same train. But it is a start, and to be encouraged.

From experience, mistakes, and a straw poll of the saner class of psychologists, here are some ways to encourage it:

- Don't try too hard. If your belovedest, oldest friend is coming for the weekend with her five-year-old, who hasn't encountered yours since both were *in utero*, it is a pretty safe bet that they will start by hating each other. The tension is just too much. Enforce common courtesy, showing them round the house and so forth, then ignore them. Don't automatically assume your own child wants to share a bedroom with some total stranger. Suppose someone said to you, 'There's another girl of thirty-two coming, that'll be fun, you can sleep in the bunks together and be together all day long.' You'd think they were mad, or that you were on a really cheap package holiday.

- Demonstrate that friendship is a good thing. When you are going to see your own friends, show obvious pleasure: talk about them eagerly, refer to them, explain if you're doing shopping as a favour for them, or they for you. Make a heroic effort not to be heard referring to 'Daddy's friends in the golf club/darts team' as if they were an unpleasant affliction. Even if they are.

- The sooner a child gets the idea of making a free and joyful choice of friend, the better. Grit your teeth. Provide your child with that 'pool of eligibles' – children the same age or thereabouts – seen fairly regularly. Before school, this entails either a playgroup or a pretty intensive round of coffee-drinking in various kitchens. Unless you live ten miles up a farm track or have accidentally settled in the middle of a block of sheltered housing for the elderly, there will be children around somewhere. It is tempting to stick to your own friends and their children, but it has to be a biggish circle. Not everyone likes the Boy Next Door all that much. We only ever had one, and I couldn't stand him.

If you consider the other children in your street 'rough', or 'unsuitable', that is a problem. It is not for me to write you off as a snob. It is indeed very annoying to have your carefully nurtured, childlike, innocent offspring coming home raving about Kylie Minogue, demanding luminous sweets and equally luminous plastic ponies done up in fetishistic plastic macs, or showing a distressing familiarity with the etiquette of 'nicking wheels' passed down from their friend's big brother who is doing two years' probation.

All you can do is reiterate your own values in a quiet, holy way and make damn sure that when the knowing little minx in the seamed stockings and ra-ra skirt comes round to your house, you make her play Animal Snap, however loudly she demands a rock video.

- On the other hand, if a friendship is going well, don't interfere. Between three and eight, children play a lot of really, really silly games. It is not your business to improve them unless bloodshed threatens.

- Don't accidentally discourage companionship. If your child is shy with other children, don't reward it by saying, 'Oh, he's Mummy's boy, always on my knee, aren't you, sweetie?' Don't make remarks to other adults which suggest that social contact is something undesirable ('Aren't they noisy when you get two of them together?') Yes, of course it's true. But say it privately.

- Martin Herbert, the best child psychologist in the universe, once wrote that 'a friendly relationship is one which requires a degree of self-awareness and social sensitivity'. Babies are not born with either quality, don't know whether they're being nice or nasty, and don't care. Gradually you teach them. 'If the immediate circle is happy, relaxed and outgoing, with plenty of love and admiration for the baby, he will have a good self-image and get on well with others.' If you are cold and formal and forever judging and disapproving, your child will become anxious and defensive, and find it hard to relax into happy-go-lucky tolerant friendships.

- Aggressive children, your own or others', are sometimes merely in need of advice on other ways to cope. They may actually not know about 'taking turns' or 'sharing' because nobody ever told them. Tell them, gently. Then tell them again. And again. And show them. Keep sharing things. Let the cat have a turn with your knitting wool, and your daughter have a turn with your lipstick. One day it will sink in.

- When school starts, try to make sure there are still contacts with some friends at other schools, or visits from scattered relations. It can be a blessed relief – for all concerned – to get out of the hothouse world of classroom friendships into something calmer and more enduring. A child who is feeling at odds with the world because George at school has deserted him will be immeasurably soothed by remembering that Jeremy – who is back from boarding school this very weekend – is keen to see him and pick up where they left off.

- Just in case you are George's mummy in the above case, don't be shocked by his fickleness. Children's friendships can be brief as a bubble, but short does not mean shallow. Don't force it. Unkindness is taboo, but fickleness isn't. If

Laura has gone off Becky, she has to be nice to Becky if she meets her, but she does not have to ask her to tea. You, on the other hand, have to smooth things over with Becky's mother. Especially since the little madams will be inseparable again in a week or so. Girls, I fear, are rather more prone to this sort of Burton–Taylor relationship than boys. Boys either fight or ignore each other or get on fine. Girls seem to practise all the nuances of relationships just for the fun of it. 'I hate you, Zoë, Mummy, I hate Zoë. She's my best friend, I hate her. I'm going to make her only my second-best friend after Sarah. Sarah, hate you!' Having a gang of little girls round for the afternoon is like living in the Miss World dressing room. I am sorry to be sexist, but it is. They – we! – grow out of it. Mostly.

15

On this subject, what about your own relationship with other people's children? It can be surprisingly nice. All new mothers know the feeling so beautifully expressed by Pam Ayres – 'It's hard to explain/When I look at your Wayne/Why you bothered to have one at all'. And which of us can say, hand on heart, that she has never looked at the pudgy, whining little brat next door and thought, ever so quietly to herself, 'Eeugh!'? Yet there is something nice about a gang of children in the house, a basketful of rowdy puppies, growing up together in a close neighbourhood. We have lost the extended family, in the West, and I rather regret it. Other people's children are fun, because you aren't deeply responsible for them and they can't wind you up into a rage the way your own can. If they are round to play, you keep them safe and prevent any real crimes, but don't particularly care if they wipe their mouth on their sleeve. On the other hand, if you fall into a cross panic trying to find everyone's wellies, your own children will resent it but the outsiders will look on fairly placidly. It is fun to give presents to other children, guessing what they want with fresh, outsiders' eyes. And if they do misbehave badly, you find it surprisingly easy to pull them up sharp: they are warier of non-parents. You get a glimmering of the answer to that great mystery of all mysteries, which is how on earth primary school teachers manage to get twenty-five children under five to sit in a row singing 'The Wheels of the Bus', when you can't seem to control your one or two.

There is, however, a double standard about disciplining other people's children. Every mother I speak to says that she hopes very much that other parents do occasionally bawl her child out for violence or destructiveness, or even bad manners, but that she feels awkward doing it herself. I used to coo and pussyfoot around other people's offspring in my uncertain days, and would go to great lengths rather than bark severely at them or withhold their pudding course. I have gradually got tougher. Once, three families together, we went on a wild windy holiday on the Norfolk Broads with nine children aged between two and ten. On the first evening the three mothers drank a cere-monial gin together and solemnly gave one another full permission to shout at or *in extremis* even slap one another's off-spring. It worked fine. Except that I did observe the rather curious law of nature which decrees that when four little boys are having social difficulties and one of them gets excluded from the gang, the mothers who keep saying 'Let them sort it out for themselves' are invariably the mothers of the three who are winning. The mother of the outcast is not so sure. Thereafter, their alliances were drawn up in no fewer than three permutations. We, and our sons, remain friends to this day. It can be done. So if you are not a natural earth mother, if you are currently rather shy and awkward with your children's peers, persevere. Anyone can get the hang of it. Occasionally, the mingling of families gives you a sense of the vast closeness of the whole human family: all children belonging to all parents. One night when her father was away on a long trip, my daughter narrowly watched a visiting Daddy giving his little girl a hug. 'May I join that hug?' she asked, and did so. He didn't replace her own father and had no ambition to, but the hug, on both sides, was very welcome. Tears sprang to my eyes. Later on, I saw the chaos they had all made of the newly tidied playroom. But I minded less than usual.

3. Mum-upmanship: Other children's parents

I have said it before, and I shall say it again: the best present you can give a pregnant woman is to introduce her to another pregnant woman who lives in the same street. We need each other. It is not a glamorous or much written-about relationship: baby-gurus confine themselves as a rule to droning on about bonding and the role of the father and how to find a good GP. They discuss siblings, and grandparents, the childminders; they worry about our children's need to 'interact' with other children. Nobody thinks about Mummy's relationships, or considers that she might fancy interacting with someone over seven years old; yet there she is, stuck at home or darting in and out to work, and she needs friends. No, more than friends: she needs fellow enthusiasts, comrades-in-arms, people who really understand. She needs *other mothers*.

She may, of course, pretend that she doesn't. I was like this. When I first stared at that miraculous brown ring on the home predictor test tube, I looked forward to the baby but dreaded the rest. I had a nasty suspicion that motherhood might involve sitting round in kitchens littered with hideous plastic toys, discussing potty-training while other people's toddlers wiped their noses on my knee. I wanted none of it. My baby and I would mix, I swore, with the same sort of friends as before: single men, working girls, old mates and colleagues. I would refuse to join a coffee circle. I didn't like mumsy women, and I didn't even like coffee much. As in so many other prenatal theories, I was comically wrong.

Society belittles mothers and babies, and it would be folly not to stick together. We become astonishingly intimate: who would have thought that you, that reserved and private person who was shy of mentioning her pregnancy, would end up within nine months discussing the shape of your nipples, your relationship with your mother and your husband's domestic deficiencies, with some girl you only met two weeks ago at the clinic? Let alone leaving your unique and precious baby in her spare room while you got a haircut?

As the years roll by, the picture changes. Mother-and-toddler groups and playgroups widen the trawl of your net, and you have more of a choice. You also start to discover the pitfalls of inter-mother comradeship. The instant intimacy which springs up between two women whose babies are sweetly hugging one another under a kitchen table can mask a lot of basic incompatibility. This has its advantages: frankly, if you are at home with a baby it is probably better to mix with the odd snob or bigot or dull doormat than with nobody at all. Everyone has their good points and there's no sense in picking fights. Soldiers in isolated barracks know that, and so do women sitting on the floor of Methodist church halls watching their babies stagger round in circles while the rain drums on the tin roof. But as babies grow into schoolchildren, the expedient friendships wither away – gently, one hopes – and the real ones develop into something else. But we still retain the instinct to put out a glad hand to another woman – any woman – with a child the same age as ours. It is an instinct that can lead us somewhat astray.

Here are the six worst enemies of sisterhood. Some of them may be you, at times. Some have been me. Spot the ones you recognize:

- *Dreary Deirdre* She is a wonderful friend to those in trouble. She looks after their children, helps change the lock against their drunken estranged husbands, cooks them meals, and listens sympathetically for hours to the chronicle of disasters. The curious thing is that she gets quite annoyed when your troubles are over, and you realize that she has been treating you as a sort of soap opera all along.

- *Sloppy Sal* You love her for being untidier than you, for letting the dog lick the plates, never combing her children's hair, carrying around three stone of postnatal flab and forgetting

19

which night is parents' evening at school. Encouraged by her example, you become even worse, until you suddenly react against her and make friends with

- *Perfect Pru* whose house is immaculate, her curtains and carpet white, and who keeps toys perfectly arranged in designer boxes. Her children never touch sweets, crisps, or anything with an E-number on the packet. So far so good: the trouble is that whenever she comes to your house she manages – in a casual way – to fire off some small but deadly request to underline your deficiencies. Like, 'Have you a needle and white thread handy?' or, 'Is there a *clean* hanky I could borrow?' If you have the nerve, lend her all the greyish hankies in the drawer. They will come back whiter than white, and ironed.

- *Defensive Dora* is hard to handle. Fun, lively and uncritical most of the time, she has a blind spot about her own child. Whenever there is fighting, biting, or a splintering crash of china, it is not her darling baby's fault. It is not even neutral: it is *your* child's fault, so there.

- *Moaning Min* on the other hand blames her children for everything, from her figure to her premenstrual tension. She comes on like a trapped bird, fluttering desperately against the bars of motherhood. She seems to get no kick from the brief anarchic fun of nursery days, and can't wait till they grow up. She radiates unhappiness, and you worry about her children. No need: having used up her misery on you, Min is a ray of sunshine at home.

- *Penny the Parasite* You never grow tired of her company, because you never see her for very long. She will pop round ostensibly to visit you, remember a bit of shopping, leave little Tarquin playing 'so sweetly, bless them' with your child, and vanish for three and a half hours. When you try to retaliate by dropping off your little Germaine for twenty minutes, she will claim that her mother is staying and has a nervous dread of non-grandchildren. However, if your child has a real friendship with hers, she might actually be the best of the bunch: you get hours of peace at home to read or write while the children amuse one another, and you don't have to drink any coffee.

Nice women, all of them, really. Enjoy them now. Another few years, and you'll be dragooned back into what they now call the 'workplace' as one of those highly trendy Women Returners. And, listening to the MD going on about golf and cash-flow, you will think nostalgically of Min and Dora. Not so, however, with the last and most dangerous type:

• *Competitive Clara* Her baby rolled, sat, teethed, crawled, walked, talked and aimed accurately at the potty before anyone else's. So she says. He is also amazingly sensitive, musical, athletic and socially well-adjusted. The entire neighbourhood hopes, with a distressing lack of charity, that one day young Victor will wet his pants and bite the class teacher to the bone. A cheer will go up from the whole street.

This business of Mum-upmanship is worth going into, if only because it blights so many happy moments and clouds so many relationships. There are two great vices which mar the fair face of motherhood. One is guilt, and the other is competitiveness. Both are rampant from the very start: maternity wards are full of women weeping guiltily because they aren't good enough at breastfeeding, while at the same time noting that none of the other babies in the ward is as good-looking and alert as their own. The fact that most of us see no contradiction in indulging these two emotions simultaneously is a great tribute to the blurring power of hormones.

Maternal guilt tends to wither away after the first few years. This is probably because as soon as your children can talk clearly, they start accusing you of being a hateful Mummy themselves, thus saving you the bother of accusing yourself. But competitiveness does not wither. Maybe it is because

Western society so worships careers, and gives mothers so little sense of personal value, that the non-earning mother is almost forced to turn her child into an award-winning, business-expansion product just in order to feel part of society. Career mothers are oddly less competitive, in my experience. They get their urge to win over with, at the office. Among most of us, competitiveness flourishes horribly.

And whereas it didn't matter too much in the early stages – babies frankly do not give a damn whether Jason down the road has got more teeth than them – as children grow older the terrible sport of Mum-upmanship does ever more harm. Normally sane, kindly women become cruel. 'Oh, Jamie's at the playgroup, is he? Well, we did look, of course, but it wasn't quite Victor's cup of tea. The driving is an awful bore, of course, but having him in the pre-pre-prep at St Bastard's has really done wonders. Their early reading scheme is marvellous, he just adores his books.' You gasp, and rally your own forces. 'Well, that's nice . . . such a comfort, especially with a child who's not too happy socially.' Victor's mother recognizes her tactical error and changes ground. 'Oh, the books are just for his quiet time indoors. He's completely fanatical about his tennis, though. It's been well worth the coaching.' And you slink off resentfully, plotting a comeback as if you were some paranoid press tycoon who has had his circulation dented. The actual children, needless to say, are pleasant little boys of five with average brains, and interests which change completely once a fortnight. If they feel competitive, they push one another over in a nice straightforward way. They do not have a problem. Their mothers do.

A primary school head once told me that he had given up using only one reading scheme, but mixes up the books from different schemes. This is not for any particular educational reason, but because he was getting so many tight-lipped mothers coming to ask him, 'Why is Rowanne only on Blue Book Two when Jackie, who's got the same birthday, is on Red Book One already?' The head would do his best to reassure her, knowing guiltily all the time that her lips would tighten even further when she discovered that Jackie is playing the

Virgin Mary in the Christmas play, and Rowanne is only a minor chorus angel. Back home, you may be sure that Rowanne's mother keeps as close an eye on the goings-on at Jackie's house as any industrial spy does on his rival. Jackie's taken the stabilizers off her bike? Right, out comes the spanner and poor old wobbly Rowanne is in for a week of grazed elbows and tears. Jackie's going to ballet class in Pineapple legwarmers? Rowanne, get your coat. We are off to be measured for a tutu. Suck in your tummy, dear. The two mothers pretend to be great friends: when they meet in the supermarket you can see their teeth glittering from the other end of the aisle.

Fathers are not exempt, either. Especially on school sports day. Woe betide the confused five-year-old who runs the wrong way, the unathletic six who can't get into his sack fast enough,

23

the poet and dreamer who is so surprised to see the tape that he stops dead within a metre of it while the field thunders by. Daddy will be out and on to his carphone within seconds, trying to book him a personal athletics coach.

All right, I exaggerate. A little. But there are thousands of us who – in short bursts of insecurity, or anxiety – willingly lock ourselves into one of the saddest, least profitable competitions in the world. Nobody will ever win. Exaggerated pride in one's own child's achievements is not a sign of love, but a lack of love. Instead of vainly hunting for reasonable explanations as to why we love our child best (because he is musical, reads faster, got more teeth sooner, is brighter and stronger) we should accept that we rate him more highly because he is our own, and that is the end of the matter. Look at the best sort of parents of severely handicapped children: theirs will never compete on any obvious level, and do they keep apologizing for them, or nervously bragging about how many steps theirs took compared to the other cerebral palsy child down the road? They do not. They just love them and help them as far as they can go. The central lesson they have learned, with some pain, is about individuality. It would do the rest of us no harm either.

4. The Dawn of Discipline: Sense, slaps and self-defence

I have not been looking forward to writing this chapter, not one bit. To use the word 'discipline' is the quickest way to rattle, disconcert, or infuriate other parents. You suspect that they think your child is either unmanageably spoilt or unnaturally repressed. You make excuses, but all the time you are thinking much the same about theirs.

For there are many styles of family life. Take one street: Mr and Mrs Careful always make the children write thank you letters, eat up their spinach, stand when a visitor enters the room and switch their reading-lights out at seven. They are not allowed to put their feet on the sofas even though they have separate indoor and outdoor shoes. Next door the children of the Reckless family dash about with uncombed hair, climb on the furniture with Wellington boots on, go to bed when they feel like it and call their parents names. However, they are avid readers and very musical. Next to them are the Grumps. Their children likewise have no bedtime, never eat at table but live on a running buffet of crisps and sausage rolls, and play in the middle of the road with a home-made go-cart constructed of all the wheels missing from local prams in the last six months.

The pecking order here is more complicated than it looks at first sight. Obviously, Mr and Mrs Careful think the other two families are appalling; on the other hand, they do slap their children quite often, which is very shocking to the Reckless family. The Recklesses never slap, nor do they let their children hit anyone: it is the only solid rule in their chaotic, artistic household. Mr Careful, on the other hand, is rather in favour of fighting – 'They've got to stand up for themselves,' he says.

The Recklesses look down on the Grumps, largely because the Grump children spend too much time watching television and kicking tin cans up and down the street. But the Grumps

25

despise the Careful children because they tell tales on each other, and the Reckless children because they use rude language. Also, the Grump children clearly have their heart in the right place: they were the only ones who went on the latest charity walk and raised money for the Save the Children Fund. The Carefuls were worried about their children getting too tired, and the Recklesses forgot the date.

The only thing which unites all six parents is a deep contempt for the Nouveaus, in the rather bigger house up the road, because they delegate the whole question of behaviour to a hired nanny and an expensive boarding school. It need hardly be said that the Nouveaus think all three of the other families are bringing up ghastly little hooligans.

With such widely diverging styles of family life, who is going to say what 'discipline' consists of? And how early do you start? There are still batty authoritarian midwives and nannies around who truly believe you can discipline a new baby – 'stick to four-hourly feeding and let her cry, dear, she's got to know who's boss'; there are even more who regularly slap children under two (pointless and unkind). You and I know they are wrong: but we also know the sort of weak-kneed family where the doctrine of demand-feeding for new babies gets extended, year by year, until they are providing demand-washing-up after spoilt teenagers, and eventually demand-lending of the family car five nights a week without thanks. We shrink from that: but on the other hand, we don't want to be ruthless disciplinarians, do we? A family, after all, is not the Chinese Army.

The word 'discipline' itself is a pitfall. Politicians bang us over the head with it whenever someone throws a beer can off a football terrace: 'No parental discipline,' they say. On the other hand, earnest schoolteachers intone platitudes about 'instilling self-discipline rather than obedience to petty rules'; while back home, fathers struggle in exhausted from the office and roar, 'That child doesn't know the meaning of discipline!' when a chippy five-year-old won't go to bed. And all the time, we are haunted by a vague Victorian bogey of merciless discipline: by Mr Murdstone and Wackford Squeers and the image of sobbing tots being shut in dark cupboards for hours.

So let us strip the humbug from the word. Discipline is a word closely allied to 'disciple'; it is about learning. It is the individual's ability to order his conduct. It needs to be taught. Get that straight; discipline is that element of good behaviour which has been instilled from outside, however gently. It is not the same thing as the natural kindness, or quietness, or interested concentration on a task which we often see in a child. There is no discipline involved when a timid child doesn't run away from Mummy in the road, if the reason he doesn't is merely that he doesn't dare to; on the other hand, the child who is fearless and curious and learns to control his impulse to dart off is worthy of high praise and reward. There is nothing necessarily 'good' about a naturally quiet child who is happy to draw pictures for hours on a long, dull train journey; he is being no better and no worse than the brat across the aisle who runs up and down and bounces on the seats. They just have different natures, and as they grow older, each will have to learn to control the instincts that nature gave him. Discipline will drive the bookish child out into the fresh air to get a bit of exercise; discipline will keep the rowdy one sitting quiet over his books to get a bit of learning.

Obeying rules is only a small part of it. Rules are necessary to keep society together and individuals safe, but real self-control goes deeper than that. What we are talking about is the process of learning three things: self-control; consideration for others; and how to wait for what you want. 'Delayed gratification', the psychologists call it. A brand-new baby has none of these things: it screams when it is hungry or uncomfortable, doesn't care what effect it has on you at three in the morning, and is incapable of waiting. Over the next five or six years, he is going to have to grow out of this screaming selfishness, and you are going to have to help. But where do you start, and how? Most parents, unless they have been teachers or scoutmasters or regimental sergeant majors, have no experience of imposing discipline on other human beings; besides, they love this little creature to death and can't bear to see it sad.

With a child under about two, there is no point at all in getting cross: you just keep on removing the forbidden thing.

27

However, when the stage comes that the child goes for the light socket while glancing over its shoulder at you, or even giggling, then you can inject a bit more steel into your tone. No violence is necessary: a really serious, fierce 'NO!' is as shocking as a slap to a baby that is used to affection. About this stage, too, comes the beginning of the vital lesson of delayed gratification. A child learns that it has to wait for its supper because you are still making it. Again, you have to gauge very skilfully whether it is worth while ticking a toddler off for whining and pestering for the food: it could be desperately hungry and totally out of control on one occasion, and on another behave the same way just as a whiny try-on. In the earlier stage, losing your temper is fatal: it frightens without teaching anything. You have to maintain a Pollyannaish sort of gently firmness, even if it means you walk out of the room occasionally and have a good swear at the cat. Once it becomes obvious that the child knows it is winding you up – usually over three years old – I personally think it does no harm to shout. Children have to learn sometime that mummies have feelings, too. But never sulk with a small child: they forgive and forget in a matter of seconds, and so must you. Frequently in our house there has gone up a cry of 'SHUT UP! Come on, pet, into the bath, whoops, there's a lovely girl!' almost in the same breath.

It helps the process of discipline if you take the trouble to explain. 'We can't got to the playground because the plumber's coming. If he doesn't come, we won't have any hot water for bathtime. No, we have to have baths, else we'd get so dirty we might get poorly,' etc, etc. It also helps if you point out something which children can't be expected to know before they start school, which is that *everyone* has to obey sets of rules. The average four-year-old is utterly fascinated by the idea of laws, police, prisons and the rest of it, and it cheers him up to think that his all-powerful parents also live under some sort of outside control. In a casual way, you can also point out when you yourself are doing something you don't particularly like in order to help someone else, 'Oh dear, better take this heavy old washing to the laundrette for Mrs Biggs next door, she's a bit poorly.' 'Better pick up all our picnic rubbish and throw it away, it wouldn't be nice for other people to find, would it?' (However, it takes a certain skill to do this without giving your child the idea that other people are nothing but a blasted nuisance. To quote the old music-hall joke: 'God put us here on earth to help others. What he put the others here for, God only knows.')

At all stages, the best guideline is to know your own child very well. My son, for example, went through an infuriating phase at four when every time we refused him anything he would shout, 'You poo-face!', and storm out of the room slamming the door. From an older child this would be grounds for chasing after him and exacting an apology ('Don't speak to your father like that!'), but what was actually happening was that a very small child was accepting a rule, stopping his demands, and then suddenly letting off steam in the only way he could think of. So we decided to overlook being called poo-faces.

In the end, the only kind of discipline worth having is self-discipline: otherwise, once the brakes are off there is nothing to stop a grown child from running wild. The offspring of dreadfully strict homes often go seriously off the rails, once Father or Mother or Nanny or Teacher is well out of sight. Self-control is the only reliable control: and you'll never have self-control until you accept the idea of 'delaying gratification'. This is exceptionally difficult to instil today, in a fairly affluent society where adults are constantly wooed by credit firms and shops to 'take the waiting out of wanting'. However far down this primrose path you have gone yourself, you owe it to your child to keep at least some of the waiting in his wanting. It doesn't have to be repressive: the good old principle of 'reinforcing good behaviour' is perfectly effective. Every time a child saves a sweet for later or waits with dignity for a birthday treat, you can let him know that you find it, and him, more special for that perseverance. If he then shares it with another child, no praise is too lavish (only do it privately, later).

Whingeing Whining, moaning, whingeing, call it what you will, it is an offence. It may well bring the average parent nearer to smacking point than many graver offences. When children are tiny is the time to begin campaigning against the 'whiny voice', making them ask for things again, in a 'nice voice'. Even if you do this religiously from the age of two, however, the sound of aggrieved whining will still be with you for some years. It is difficult to know how to treat it, since its only real fault is that it drives you, personally, mad. I dislike the system some people have of pretending the child has changed identity. 'Oh, where's Timmy? There's a horrid little boy come instead who whines. I wish Timmy would come back . . .' There is something creepy about this popular line. However, I have at times resorted very successfully to a claim that my ears have been fitted with 'whine filters', so that I actually cannot hear demands made in a complaining tone of voice. With a bit of convincing acting from the parent, a child will half-believe this – he knows it isn't real, but acts as if it were. It is also a bit of a joke, and saves resorting to punishments or antisocial roaring.

Eating   If there is one truly futile battle in this area, it is the battle over 'eating up'. Eating should not be a matter of virtue or naughtiness: only fuel or pleasure. Children use odd eating habits as a lever to annoy parents, but they also have genuine oddities of preference. Either way, do not rise to provocation. A lump of brown bread and peanut butter followed by a bit of fruit is a balanced meal. So are many other combinations and snacks. The only actual rules worth trying to enforce over food are: no junk between meals except on special days, and no sweet or pudding until you've had some protein and something green. Try not to scream aloud when your child goes to a friend's house and keenly tucks in to meat-and-two-veg he wouldn't touch at home; try not to be neurotic about junk food at parties and on outings. In 99 per cent of cases it does no harm as an occasional treat, however depressed you may get at the luminous orange stain around your child's mouth.

Smacking   Here the ways divide. Some countries already ban all parental smacking; Britain is undergoing a furious debate as to whether we should follow suit. Everyone except a few mad old floggers is in broad agreement that you shouldn't hit babies or tiny toddlers, that you should never give more than one sharp slap, and that you should in no circumstances, ever, hit a child on the head, or with an instrument – stick, spoon or strap. But a vociferous lobby still demands that 'any hostile physical act against a child' *including restraint*, should be illegal. I have done quite a few interviews on the subject, and the main proponents of this idea, I would like to tell you, have teenage or adult children and distinctly short memories. When you try to describe what it is actually like living with a stroppy four- or five-year-old, they merely look blank. But the arguments have been fascinating to follow. Basically, the case against smacking is:

- It doesn't work.

- It leads on to harder hitting, even child abuse.

- It is symbolic of a bad attitude to children, that they have less than full human rights. We don't hit prisoners, or even murderers, any more.

The alternative that they suggest is to 'reason' with the child, or to 'withdraw your approval' – a pompous phrase.
The case for smacking is:

- It does sometimes work.

- It doesn't need to lead on to harder hitting. For every thousand families where children are occasionally smacked, perhaps one descends towards real violence.

- Mother cats do it all the time. It is not symbolic of anything, but instinctive and as natural a part of mothering as a cuddle. It is a good way for children to learn that they can drive you that bit too far.

Advocates of the odd smack also point out that 'reasoning' can turn into remorseless nagging, and that 'withdrawing approval' can cover all sorts of chilly mental cruelty. Remember the nasty

31

aunt in the Saki story, who whenever one child transgressed, would invent a new treat for all the others from which the criminal would be excluded. Children are impulsive, dramatic beings and as the writer Lynette Burrows put it, 'the brief spirited drama of a slap' can knock them back on course a great deal faster and less depressingly than endless nagging. I have

How did you stop yours spitting?

slapped my children now and then, and its main virtue is that it sometimes brings a rapid end to an episode which would, under any other system, have lingered unpleasantly on. 'I said you *don't* kick your sister and you *don't* spit at people', accompanied by not particularly violent swipes across the bottom can sometimes seem a better solution than: 'Now then, you mustn't kick, you know that – how would you like it if she kicked you? She did kick you? And take your car? Well, she's a lot younger and you should have told me, not kicked back . . . no, you mustn't spit, it isn't nice – no, it isn't, don't be cheeky or no pudding for you at lunchtime – Frederick, you must never ever call me that again. Go to your room.'

If Frederick will not go to his room, his mother will have to shout, or take him by force (restraint might be illegal, though, remember?). By lunchtime he will have forgotten what he did, and withdrawing his pudding will seem a very petty and nasty thing to do. He will feel a vague, generalized resentment all day. If you had lovingly, exasperatedly, slapped him (and then given back the car his wretched sister stole) the whole thing would have been over in seconds. OK, you have affronted his dignity as a human being, but at least in his mind kicking and spitting will forever be associated with a loss of personal dignity.

But whatever you think – and there are half a dozen other valid ways of handling the tiresome little scenario above – the real damage done by the anti-smacking campaigners has been to the already low self-esteem of mothers. Frankly, most of us are driven to a smack now and then: either instinct tells us it is right, or weariness and exasperation make us do it – not very hard – to relieve our own feelings. So when respected child-care gurus say smacking is a bad, bad, wicked thing and 'invariably' leads on to child abuse, we panic. Our instincts are all wrong! We are Bad Mothers! We always suspected we were, from the very first moment our natural childbirth turned into a forceps drama. We are cruel harridans, who need the Law to keep us in order. It takes very little, especially in the cold Nordic cultures, to make mothers feel wretchedly inadequate: and it does no good. From what I have seen in normally loving families, what happens is that there is a short phase – from about three to five – when smacking happens naturally. After five a child begins to develop a certain additional dignity, and somehow you hesitate to shatter that with a smack. If you are still smacking a seven-year-old, it is worth reconsidering matters. For one thing, he or she is more amenable to reason, bribes and threats. You can withdraw privileges by now without being unfair, simply because of the child's longer memory: once my children started getting pocket money, I could use fines to great effect. (Kicking and spitting are now 5p per offence. But I am not heartless. You can win back your 5ps by deeds of great kindness, helpfulness and consideration.)

Other punishments are various, and depressing to list: deprivation of television, of treat food, sending to bedrooms, banning friends coming round for a week, and so on. The only thing to say about any sort of punishment is STOP IT FROM ESCALATING. All human conflict has a fatal tendency to spiral upwards if it is not stopped by one strong-minded participant: that is how smacking turns into beating, and reasoning turns into mental cruelty. Usually parents stop it getting out of control: it is when they use the power of parenthood to vent emotions which are not much to do with the actual child, that disasters occur. Whatever you do, don't let things escalate. If for some reason you are alone and friendless, or feel it; if your rebukes are turning into furious shouting half the day; if the pocket money fines reach weeks ahead and you lash out mindlessly before considering the justice of the case, then take a grip on yourself.

Get out of the room, brush your hair, give yourself a small treat. Look at the photographs of your tormentor as a beloved baby, and cry if you feel like it. Then look at the present and realize how well you have actually done so far, to raise a child healthy and bonny and bright and defiant. Even the defiance is a tribute to loving and non-violent upbringing.

And if you have reached such a catharsis of unhappiness and conflict, remember something else. Love is better than justice. Having a punishment cancelled out of love is not, as some would claim, a sure recipe for a spoilt child. It can be the best lesson of all. Never mind that the little demon got clean away with breaking the bathroom mirror in a temper, ripping up a new book or calling you a stupid old cow for the fifteenth time in a morning: if you have had a dreadful row, then have the grace sometimes to drown resentments in a hug and a laugh. Even apologize for your own temper. How else can a child learn to do the same?

5. Television: Is there a cure?

Of all the dreadful, guilt-inducing sights for a caring parent, few are worse than the sight of a bright, keen, good-hearted and impressionable little child sitting mesmerized by some appalling cynical rubbish on the television screen. Modern children watch too much television: sometimes four or five hours a day, or even more, and it is a disgrace to all of us. One resignedly expects teenagers to lie around like slugs all day watching nonsense while the sun shines vainly outside: it is part of the mysterious process of modern puberty. But for a five- or six-year-old to be passive, uncritical and vague, sitting waiting for the next bit of trite or violent programming to be piped into his head, is a dreadful thing indeed.

So what do you do? Especially if you are a daddy? You get crosser and crosser at their passivity, and finally storm in to the room shouting, 'Turn off that rubbish!' and arousing bitter resentments in the bosom of your little ones. They regard you, quite rightly, as an inconsistent great bully. Quite possibly the programme they were watching was a perfectly intelligent documentary about seabirds, even if it did follow thirty-five minutes of obscenely bulging American superheroes zapping one another in the name of intergalactic brotherhood. You didn't interrupt that one because you were busy talking about an intricate problem on the phone, and preferred distant spaceship noises to close-up whingeing of 'I'm bored, what can I do?' That is no excuse. What you lacked, Dad, what we have all lacked at times, was a Clear Policy.

To assist you in forming one, here is a set of guidelines. Some are my own family's, some borrowed, some frankly verging on the fanatical. Pick a few, formulate a policy, and stick to it:

- Accept from the outset that some television is good for children. There are dramas, stories, documentaries, well-made cartoons and children's news programmes which make a positive contribution to their education. Let them know that you approve, and watch with them sometimes, uttering constructive criticisms. There is no point in regarding television as a mere vice. Taking the good from it is the first step towards rejecting the bad or banal.

- Make a rule – from earliest years – that they always switch off the machine at the end of a programme, so that they can discuss it. Even when our children are allowed to see two consecutive programmes, they still switch off for a moment in between. In this way, television is treated like a book, or a meal properly set at table: something to approach deliberately and intelligently rather than used as a non-stop tap of indifferent, half-understood entertainment.

I'm curious about the mindless violence involved

one has to consider the genre in which the programme was originally created

- If you can possibly afford a video recorder, get one. Use it to tape and keep programmes for children. Watching the same thing twice or three times doesn't hurt: it encourages a critical attitude. Even a five-year-old will start to wonder how the puppets move, or why they put a song in the play just there: raising a new generation of critics has to be better than a generation of couch potatoes. A video also enables you to enforce time rules, such as no television before lunch, ever. And yes, it lets you use the television sometimes as a babysitter – when you are desperate for peace and quiet with a newspaper in the next room – because you can know that they are watching something worth seeing, which you have vetted.

- If a child really wants to watch a programme you regard as pointless rubbish (probably because everyone else in school does), a good compromise is to agree provided that he subsequently switches off and writes a review (minimum 40 words) and draws a picture to illustrate it. The labour of spelling out the plot of 'WonderBarbie meets My Little Pony' may well dent its appeal.

- Encourage a child to distinguish between programmes that make her think and tell her new things, and what my children call 'the brainlesses'. Everyone is entitled to one or two brainlesses a week, but they ought to know which ones they are. Mine is Coronation Street.

- Watch with them for at least one session a week, and try to gauge how much they do and don't understand, especially of advertising. Explain what advertising is for, and how it tries to persuade you to want things. Analyse techniques (four is not too young to start). Children rather like to be one up on the adult world, and rapidly stop wanting advertised toys so much when they have understood that someone is trying to trick them into desire.

- Try to put off for as long as possible teaching young children how to switch on the television by themselves. I never fail to be amazed at the way some children of three and four will hammer downstairs at dawn to switch on pappy Breakfast

TV. Switch the thing off at the mains, put a chair in front of the switch, don't make it easy. Having said that, one very enterprising small child I know came down one morning alone, switched on the TV, didn't think much of the pictures and boldly replaced them with his own, with poster paints on the screen. His parents couldn't bring themselves to scold him, since he had shown such sturdy independence of the broadcasting industry. He had, they felt, the right spirit.

6. Fair's Fair: Quibbling siblings

In the days of big families, children grew up knowing from an early age that life is unfair. It was clear to the merest toddler that some people are bigger than others, get their clothes brand new instead of handed down, and are allowed penknives. In a family of four or more children, the laws of probability dictate that at least one other child seems to have had a better birthday than you, and that someone else is, in turn, furiously jealous of yours. The laws of common sense and economics prevent every child having precisely the same present at the same time as all the others. A certain competitive spirit grows up, curiously combined with fraternal warmth: it is noticeable in later life that the sons and daughters of big families make friends easily, but also that they eat much faster than only children: this is because they spent their formative years desperate to get to the second helpings first before the food ran out.

However, in the modern two- or three-child family things are different. It is perfectly possible for the parents of two children close in age to treat them almost exactly the same from the day the youngest reaches three. If one gets a small present, the other can have an identical one. They can both go to the film, or the swimming pool, or the shops with you. They can be given equal pocket-money from quite early on, bought clothes and shoes simultaneously, and even given small presents on the other one's birthday. Father Christmas generally brings them stockings with the exact same number and quality of presents in each.

This happened for some time in our family, to the point that one child became furious at the discovery that she couldn't share the other one's godmother, and he in turn became irritated when she got a plaster on her arm and he didn't (well, his wasn't broken). Around this time I began to suspect that I had fallen into a very shaming trap. It had been a stupid if well-meant policy from the start. Identical treatment of non-identical children is a tempting line to take, but its only sure results are pretty negative: to wit, a houseful of discarded broken toys and decorations (because only one of them was really old enough for a decorated toy gondola when we got back from Venice), and a habit of watching the other's fortunes with an even more obsessive jealousy than otherwise. One friend recalls that when her older one was starting to learn the recorder at school, the girl was naturally bought a recorder. Her sister, too young to learn, took it very personally, and in vain did her mother protest that she had had a leotard and ballet-shoes for the dancing class which her sister didn't want to go to. The habit of absolute equality was there, ingrained, and every small breach of it was an outrage. 'It's not fai-yur!' Having learned this lesson the silly way, we now try negotiated settlements over different treatment ('If he has fish and chips on the way home from his maths lesson, you can have them on Thursday while he's at Matthew's . . . if I buy him the rails for his railway, I'll take you to the Care Bears film he doesn't want to see . . .')

But this obvious and closed-circuit competition is one of the reasons, I think, why sibling quarrels and the eternal debilitating chorus of 'Mu-um! He hit me!' have been in no way alleviated by the shrinking of the average family. If you have six children, you have running fights in different permutations: if you have only two, then you have intense, and possibly even more poisonous, bilateral battles. Bickering of this kind is more infuriating than anything else children do: worse than destructiveness, untidiness, cheek, defiance, lying. It brings you closer to violence, probably, than anything else. After all your efforts, these children you have borne sound bratty, spoiled, ungrateful, spiteful and petty. I now know why my own childhood was punctuated by cries of 'I'll bang your heads together!' (not that they ever did). I too have wanted to bang heads together. Yes, recently. Ten minutes ago, if you must know. Were it not for God's precious gift of alcohol, I might not be at this moment calm enough to type.

However, in a mellower mood I must admit that there are

advantages to the situation. Sooner or later, all children have
to learn about conflicts of interest. Direct conflicts with parents
are not the best way to learn: parents, after all, hold too many
trump cards and you are emotionally too dependent upon them.
Fights with outside friends are also problematical: your
opponents may diffuse the situation by going away completely,
and ending the fight with no product but cold mutual dislike.
But sibling battles are much better: when you fight with a
brother or sister, you are competing on fairly level terms with
someone who will never go away. A sib can never utterly defeat
you, yet will never entirely give in either. So these sibling battles
are the perfect parable of the wider world: of border warfare,
professional rivalry, marriage itself. They *have* to end in re-
conciliation, because otherwise neither of you can carry on a
decent existence: and the lesson of how to end them smoothly
is one which stays with you for life.

Look at the problems positively – difficult, when the back of
your car sounds like a chimp house – and the quarrels become
more bearable. They count, so you tell yourself between gritted
teeth as you swing round the wrong corner up a one-way street,
as vital social education. At the same time, your parental job
becomes more awesome. You have to represent the universal
spirit of Justice, Mercy, and Peace. You are a Kissinger, a Solomon. Bring sense and calm to this debate, and you are producing peacemakers and arbitrators for the world's stormy future.
If the idea makes you crash the gears and clip a traffic bollard,
I should stop if I were you and do some deep breathing. In
fact, what I generally do when the car is the scene of the row
is precisely that: I find a turn-off or a safe lay-by, pull up, switch
off the engine and any music tape that might be running, fold
my arms and refuse to move until the cursing and kicking
abates. It may require a bit of prompting as to how they shall
best end it, but it is worth the trouble: 'Look, if you can't agree
on whether to listen to Postman Pat or the music, we shan't
have either. Would one of you like to do a swap, and have
their choice tomorrow?' Or 'If it's actually Rose's book, let's
accept that it's Rose's. But if it's Nicholas who's reading it, it
won't do Rose any good to rip it in half will it?' Stopping the

car also enables you to fulfil the essential role of every arbitrator, which is to listen. Terry Waite once told me that the essence of his job – which was for years successful before he was kidnapped – was to sit nodding sympathetically while even the most deluded, fanatical terrorists expounded their world view. Same with you. Something may underlie this silly fight over a plastic dinosaur, and it is something you should probably know about.

I set the sample fight in a car because in a car you cannot use the classic parental cure for quarrels, which is to shout, 'Now SEPARATE! Tom upstairs, Lucy downstairs, but separate!' This has some usefulness, especially if the children need one another to play with, because in the end they will learn the vital lesson that if you want human company, you have to stop kicking it on the shins. But the more intense approach – the family conference to analyse and solve the actual quarrel – is more intensely educational. If you can face it. And in a car (or a holiday flat), believe me, you have to.

Here are some of the things siblings fight about:

Possessions You can avert a lot of these fights by having a clear and steady policy about ownership. Every child has a right to certain things of her very own, an inner core of sacrosanct objects. She should be defended to the hilt if her private drawer or cupboard is invaded. If she knows that this will happen, she is less likely to abuse the privilege by pinching someone else's things and putting them in her private drawer.

Some possessions, however, are of dubious ownership. The stone looking like an owl which one of them found on the beach, but you can't remember which; the jointly-owned box of Lego; the construction kits they both got and mixed the pieces up. If there really is no way of knowing for sure which one is claiming correctly, the Solomon solution may work – that is, take it away completely and see which one is most outraged. But it is better to persuade the children, in a rather calm, bored way, that neither of them can enjoy it while they are fighting, so they'd better work out a compromise. If you notice that one child is giving in all the time, or always producing a peace formula that costs him or her the advantage in these fights, then note it: and later lavish private praise and understanding, explaining that you know how difficult it is and that you're proud of the sensibleness being shown.

If you are preaching the message that there is no disgrace in giving some ground, don't forget to demonstrate it too. Show occasionally that even parents are susceptible to calm, sensible arguments. If you are doctrinaire and inflexible about – say – an exact bedtime even on holiday, what is there to suggest to a child that he shouldn't be equally doctrinaire about not letting his sister play gently with his train?

Dignity Young children have a great deal of personal dignity. A great many fights arise because the other child, at a loss for something to do with the morning, has jeered 'fatty', or 'bum-face' or 'crybaby'. Unfortunately, by the time the decibel level rises high enough to bring you to the scene, the accused child is also letting off a flood of invective, and both sides may well be claiming, 'He started it.' If one of them says something revealing like, 'Well, she started it by *being* a bum-face,' then you know where you are. Mention to the offender that you can see who started it, and do no more. If it remains doubtful who is persecuting whom, then you have two choices. Either deliver your message about how peace and harmony is more fun than fighting, warn that the first one to escalate into violence will be severely dealt with, and retire. Or, if things are really miserable, work out a way of separating the children. Siblings, like spouses, can get seriously on one another's nerves through too much proximity.

You This is the tricky one. Sometimes your attention and time are rationed by work pressures, or social whirls, or illness, or general depression. (All mothers get depressed at times. It is no disgrace.) When this happens, the children almost invariably make it worse by fighting over you, with wailing cries of 'It's not fai-yur!' whenever you do anything at all for one child. In this mood, children grill you as to which one you love best: the answer is, I suppose, 'Which of your eyes do you love best?

Which of your ears? Which foot?' At this stage, it is quite important to ignore my grumpy strictures against identical treatment at the start of this chapter, and preserve a scrupulous fairness in material things. But you know the real answer: try to clear the pressures, drop the commitments, let down the outsiders, and be kinder to your own beleaguered self: only so will you have enough left at the end of the day to give to your children, both or all of them.

Through all pacification and negotiation, the essential lessons to get over are:

- Quarrelling is unproductive. Arguments only work if both sides listen.

- If a fight becomes more significant than the object fought over, it is time to wind it down. Real matters of principle are rare.

- Very few objects are worth destroying a happy relationship for.

- Peace with honour is always possible.

there's no disgrace if you want to back down Mum

7. Coaching Days: Classes, courses, push and shove

Sarah Ferguson, Duchess of York, was put on to a horse when she was two. She swam at three, and skied at four. Some children play the violin by the Suzuki method at three, others sail little Optimist dinghies around with confidence on their fifth birthdays. Tennis or motorcycle training can start at four, and I have seen chunky little pre-school figures in white canvas pyjamas throwing one another about on a judo mat.

All together now: *So what?* If you joined in that cry with confidence, skip this chapter. You are a well-adjusted parent with a certain grainy confidence in your own methods. However, if – like the majority of us – you began to twitch with nervous guilt during that first paragraph, and looked outside at your own children charging one another with plastic swords or throwing stones at the wall in a seriously unstructured manner, you need to confront the issues. Many parents, under social pressure, rush around getting their children into countless 'courses' and coaching-sessions in much the same way as owners of dubious old cars keep buying cheap bolt-on accessories, go-faster stripes and flashy aerodynamic spoilers.

'Oh,' they say, meeting rival mothers, 'Nicky's absolutely loving his tennis coaching, but of course it's the Tae-Kwon-Do which is so marvellous for developing coordination before the ski season, and I think it helps his cello, too.' The other mother responds instantly. 'Well, it's the swimming that's so serious for Samantha just now, and what with Suzuki on Wednesdays and gymnastics on Thursdays, I'm not sure that it wouldn't cut too much into her riding time. She'll be hunting this winter.' Nicky and Samantha are four and five respectively, and their parents ought to be ashamed of themselves. In a couple of years, these two overloaded tots are going to be victims of a syndrome which teachers in prosperous areas are starting to report. One city teacher told me, 'I get kids who can hardly keep their eyes open at assembly, and they aren't the ones who help in the family shop either. It's the gang who never get an afternoon without an extra-curricular activity. Middle-class victims.'

Parents who let their children be over-coached in serious sporting activities are a special case: experts in sports medicine are alarmed by the number of burnt-out ten-year-olds in fields like skating or gymnastics. But there is a parallel and less visible problem of infants being overloaded with activities, perfectly good in themselves but adding up to fatigue and bewilderment in children who have lost the art of entertaining themselves by mucking about, dressing-up, and devising long, wonderful imaginative games together. Children taught specific skills in groups become competitive and develop pecking orders with chilling rapidity. They know who is best at 'it', and value them accordingly. Children in a mixed group amusing themselves have a different system: in the freer and more original atmosphere of ordinary play every child contributes a different talent. 'Matthew's brilliant at drawing machines, but I'm best at inventing what they're for. Rose can get right up the climbing frame and pull things up, because Sally's good at tying knots at the bottom.' Which group is learning most and likely to be happiest?

So take a deep breath and say to yourself the first mantra: *Six is soon enough to start anything.* For some activities, seven or eight is soon enough, and for some children all special skills – even sports with rules – can wait a good deal longer.

There are exceptions to the six-year-old rule, and they are obvious and natural. Swiss and Scandinavian mountain children learn to ski as soon as they can walk, because it is the natural family thing to do. Horsy families always plonk their children on ponies as soon as they can sit up; sailing families give the tiller to the toddler as a matter of course and lucky families with swimming pools tend to have rather young swimmers in them. The point is that none of these parents are doing it because they think it is educational, or desirable, or smart. The snow and the fat old pony and the boat are there, and the children want to copy their parents in the same way that they make cars out of cardboard boxes.

Where the special skills become suspect is when they are part of social ambition, or of the boring modern pressure on parents to 'develop' their children incessantly and by force: it is almost as if they were trying to build on a kitchen extension or a conservatory, striving as they are to increase the 'value' of their small child by having it taught a set of adult skills.

Examining my own conscience over the years, I have devised a set of awkward questions to ask yourself:

- Does my child *want* to do it? Has he/she shown the faintest aptitude or interest – patted a horse, built a toy boat in the garden, been rapt by classical music on the radio, danced since she could walk?

- Is it possible that I secretly want to be four years old again and go to the class myself?

- Has this plan got anything – *anything* – to do with the fact that the sport in question is rather chic and trendy?

- Has this plan got anything at all to do with the fact that my neighbour put her Jason in the class and claims he got a bronze medal in it last month?

- Or has it anything to do with the fact that I long for an hour off from child minding on Wednesdays, so am craftily disguising it as education undertaken for the child's sake?

As long as you know the answers, you can decide. If you do, here are some fruits of assorted mothers' experiences:

Swimming Lessons Clearly a good thing. However, once the child can swim adequately over and under water, he or she may lose interest in formal lessons and prefer mucking about with siblings (loosely supervised by you) to formal training. Stock up on ointments for verrucae and athlete's foot.

Riding Lessons If the child doesn't like it *a lot*, then stop immediately. It is too expensive and dangerous for unwilling amateurs to carry on. Never mind that you have spent £100 on clothes and hat. Sell them.

Skiing Lessons Same principle. Some love it, some hate it. There is no disgrace in reverting to a sledge.

Sailing Lessons Same principle. Buy the child a neoprene wet-suit before you start: a cold wet child can't concentrate. I would never start a child sailing until he or she *begged* to do it, because I sail myself and I am thirty-nine years old and sometimes I *still* hate it.

I know you're dying to have tennis lessons Darling —

Skating, Motocross, Tennis and sundry sports If the club concerned doesn't allow single trial lessons, don't consider it.

Music Lessons A different principle applies: it is worth continuing even when a child claims to be fed up, because there is often a breakthrough after several months. If it still doesn't happen, give up for a while and go to some good concerts instead. The world needs concert-goers as much as musicians.

Drama Classes Watch at least two before you enrol. There are some pretentious idiots running drama classes for four-year-olds which are an utter waste of time; and some brilliant, life-enhancing, happy classes too.

Dancing Classes Very good for developing discipline, co-ordination and an ability to point one's toes to order. For some strange reason, children fresh out of a dancing class are always in a dreadful temper, and kick their mothers. Something to do with relaxation of discipline, I suppose. Keep them in ballet-shoes until the mood passes.

As with so much else, arranging coaching is a matter of keeping balance and a sense of humour. And above all, a sense of your own child's individuality: a few children don't like being taught *at all*. And a few of those turn out, to everyone's surprise, to be geniuses in disguise.

8. Widening the Circle: Bachelors and baby-sitters

The first three years of parenthood are devilishly hard work, but there is a rather soothing, sheltered quality about them nonetheless. In retrospect, anyway. The outside world recedes a little way. One may complain about doors too narrow for double buggies, or restaurants that hate children, but on the whole one lives and travels in a cosy, frantic little nursery bubble of buggies and wet-wipes, teddies and tears and damp, grubby, chubby little arms around one's neck. I look now at friends whose children are under four, and rather envy them this private world: they smile, harassed, but happy, through clouds of talcum powder, wiping away tears and turning aside tantrums with a hug and a joke. Their children ask easy, if rather wearing questions, like, 'What is dat?', and fall asleep suddenly, like cats.

And you, however tired you may be, are in charge. You have created a world for them, an ambience and a moral framework within which they live more or less contentedly. But the time comes, at the age of four or five, when the child turns outwards from the family and towards the wider world. He has friends you don't know, at school or nursery. I have never forgotten the shock when my son aged five, walking through the village, suddenly waved delightedly at a lady across the road. 'GOOD MORNING, MRS SAXBY!' he bellowed. She was one of the school helpers, and I didn't know her, at that time, from Eve. But it was a shock of pleasure, in part; to see one's child turning outwards towards the big world is a mixed, bittersweet joy but a joy nonetheless. Parents, after all, do not hang around forever. Nor should we. A sort of emotional weaning now takes place; it is the moment for which the baby was rehearsing when it used to turn away from your breast in a crowded railway carriage to beam hugely at all the other passengers (leaving you horribly exposed, but then babies have no consideration). It is fun, but needs a bit of careful handling.

So who are these other adults your child will meet? First of all:

Baby-sitters The odds are that while your children were very small, you had a small circle of well-known baby-sitters. Grannies, aunts, trusted neighbours, a child minder or a nanny. Such sitters are as precious as gold dust: women with new babies suddenly find themselves taking a new interest in certain sectors of the population, covetously eyeing up motherly, widowed ladies in the supermarket and evaluating the local teenage girls with as much interest – if differently focused – as the local teenage boys do. Good baby-sitters are worth their weight in gold. Bad ones mean a disaster at best and a tragedy at worst. The most important thing about any baby-sitter is his or her brain: don't look at the punk hair, the miniskirt or the chewing gum: look for intelligence. After all, only a very wicked person would knowingly let a child come to harm, but a stupidly well-meaning one is every bit as dangerous, and far more common. If your friend's teenage daughter (or your cleaner's aunt or whoever) looks seriously gormless to you, then don't let her baby-sit *even for half an hour*, even while you go next door. One of the prime signs of real stupidity is not knowing when to call for help; another is the tendency to panic and throw water on to a burning chip pan, or waste time trying to make a poisoned child vomit, or laboriously telephoning parents and getting them called out of the cinema when it would be obvious to the meanest intelligence that the only number worth dialling is 999. A good baby-sitter is not only friendly and fun, but has a sufficiently morbid imagination to stop a child of any age going to bed cuddling a length of strangly rope, or to pick up a plastic bag blowing around on the bedroom floor. He or she will also disbelieve your child's wide-eyed, candid assurances that he is always allowed to suck boiled sweets in bed.

When children are old enough for social chat, a baby-sitter becomes an event, something to look forward to. Teenagers are highly glamorous beings to young children, and new adults of all ages represent a bracing challenge. 'Hello, Suzy. Are you a teenager? Do you go to discos? Shall we have a disco here? Would you tell us a story? Do you want to see my acrobatics? Do you want to see the bubble trick that Rose can do with her straw if you give her a drink?' Faced with a nice, kind, cosy, middle-aged lady, small boys in particular like to test the boundaries of her tolerance in the same way that horses go round a new field, leaning on all the fences to see if they are electric. I have a friend who left her two perfectly nice little boys, aged seven and five, with a new baby-sitter for one hour in the afternoon, by way of a test. She returned to find the house upside-down, drawers emptied, toys scattered, furniture upturned, rude words written on slips of paper everywhere and the baby-sitter looking vague and worried while the boys rampaged. She was cross with the children, but equally cross with the baby-sitter. You have to know when to slam the brakes on, and have the confidence to do it: someone who was wonderful with your baby may come back three years later and be a disaster.

On the other hand, over-strict baby-sitters sometimes make children reluctant to let you go out at all. It is not easy to gauge what exactly is going on, not least if you have a hyperbolic child. 'Mummy,' says the little girl, 'Katy is dreadfully cruel to us.' Mummy panics inwardly, envisaging child abuse and all manner of horrors. 'Yes, darling, what does she do?' she asks as calmly as possible. Child announces, 'Well, I apsley *hate* her. She does awful things to me.' Mummy – shovelling down Valium – 'What, darling?' 'Well,' says the child, pleased to have such close attention, 'I was getting undressed for bathtime and she told me to put my vest in the dirty-basket. She said I had to pick it up myself. And she said she wouldn't get my rubber duck off the shelf unless I picked it up.' Half an hour's questioning having failed to elicit any further evidence of unnatural cruelty, Mummy decides to leave Katy on the baby-sitting list after all.

The greatest bugbear of parents seems to be the Mating Pair of baby-sitters. They spend the evening with an uncomfortable vision of Katy and Jason snogging passionately while the children shriek for help. A friend who lives in an area where you can't get baby-sitters unless they bring their boyfriend too (largely for protection) offers the following rule-of-thumb: 'Check up with the parents. If your house is the *only* place where Katy and Jason are going to be alone, don't do it. If the teenagers have plenty of other chances to chew one another's ears, then risk it. A nice girl who is a safe baby-sitter isn't going to turn into a monster just because she's got a bit of company. Only do listen to what your children say about them afterwards.'

Baby-sitters come into your own house and become honorary, temporary, family members. The next level of outside society that impinges on a child is:

Parents of Friends Easy, this one: from babyhood onwards most children get quite accustomed to staying for hours, meals, occasionally nights at their friends' houses. The first 'sleepover' is a vast adventure, involving bagfuls of furry animals, special cuddlies, last-minute misgivings and whispered instructions to the other mummy about lavatory habits. The home-based mummy tends to sit by the telephone all evening in an agony of concern. Some children sleep happily at their friends' houses at the age of two or three; others never pluck up the nerve until seven. But it is a godsend to be able to hand a child over for the night – not only does it ease the baby-sitting problem for very late nights, but it means you have easy and untraumatic cover for any emergency that might befall you or another child and involve a night in hospital. It is good for children's morale, too: after a night at a cosy friend's house they come back with a swagger you can see from the other end of the path. Ways to smooth the way to a trustful sleepover are:

- Only do it with parents whom you and your child know pretty well. Don't ignore any signs that your child actually dislikes or fears a certain daddy, or mummy, even if you know for sure there is no sinister reason. Everyone has a right to their dislikes.

- Tell the other mother every detail of your child's idiosyncrasies: lambskin fleece, teddy bear under the head, light on the landing, pyjama jacket on back to front, dry cornflakes for breakfast, whatever. But don't be offended if the child amazes everyone by not caring about any of it after all.

are you **sure**
Mummy gives
you a gin+tonic
to "settle you down"?

- Pass on any current fears or nightmare subjects. It is very reassuring to a child when a comparatively strange adult seems perfectly *au fait* with his feelings about Rottweilers, trapdoors suddenly opening, or Nu-killer explosions.

- If you say you will be there straight away after breakfast, or even before it, *be* there. One betrayal may mean a whole year before he tries again.

When it is your turn to be the hostess, remember:

- Leave lights on all the way to the lavatory

- Remember that even the toughest and most macho little boy likes to be offered, at least, a bedtime kiss. Even if it is just so he can say 'Eeugh! Not likely' and get a laugh from his friend in the other bed.

- If your child and the visitor decide to share a bed, or lay out mattresses on the floor and camp, or practise some other eccentricity, then give it a trial. This is an exercise in independence, after all. Don't fuss.

- Don't do it before a schoolday if you can help it.

Beyond the cosy circle of home and school and Other Mummies, there is the wider world. In my view, the wider and more eccentric a child's circle of acquaintances the better. I do not see that there is any advantage for a child in growing up with the belief that everyone in the world is married, has children about his age, and belongs to the same social class. It is not too difficult to present a child with a never-ending procession of old ladies, new babies, and other children with their parents; but there are other sections of humankind too. With a cautious parental eye in the middle distance, young children can make great friends with elderly men, teenagers, the eccentric, the single, the mentally handicapped, nuns and monks, restless travellers and gays and lesbians. Within the family, some of the best relationships are between children and their bachelor uncles and aunts, who make no concessions to the cosy child-centred world but introduce a wholly welcome element of mayhem, irresponsibility and fun ('Aunt Susie,' wrote one child, 'always brings us things like bubblegum-flavour lip ice or jam from aeroplanes. Once when we had a meal at Covent Garden we couldn't find a parking space so we parked on a double yellow line and every five minutes me or Susanna had to go out and check there wasn't a traffic warden about. She paid us five pence every time we checked. She's a super aunt!')

In a well-regulated, well-disciplined, caring and responsible family there is nothing quite like a bachelor uncle or friend, found unexpectedly tucked up on the sofa in the morning with a crashing hangover but still willing to teach a nephew how to make a banana into a convincing model of a pig being sick. Some of the happiest memories of childhood in autobiographies seem to concern friendships with tramps or eccentric relatives. Now that the extended families have dispersed, there is a real risk of bringing a child up too bland, too safe, too utterly Mothercare. The soul, as well as the body, requires roughage.

A lot of these friendships need, I repeat it, middle-distance parental supervision. Perverts and paedophiles do exist; and even the moral philosophy lessons dispensed by a certain class of bachelor uncles may need a bit of discreet counterbalancing ('My uncle Neddy,' a child once remarked to a horrified acquaintance of mine, 'told me the rule of Life was, Never nick a thing you can't flog. I don't think Jesus would ip-prove of that, do you?'). But their importance is vast. Apart from anything else, the niceness of unlikely people does help to compensate for the depressing modern need to warn children constantly about:

Strangers It is axiomatic that children, growing independent, should be told not to talk to strangers. It is also very sad; in more innocent times, lonely old people in parks could chatter happily to children, telling them their life story and enjoying harmless casual friendships. Some parents consider that it is enough merely to tell children never to *go* with strangers, especially in a car; but expert opinion is that it won't do. A friendly child who has been drawn into conversation, harmlessly, perhaps more than once, is going to forget that this person is technically a 'stranger'. The only safe rule is no talking at all, unless a parent or guardian is present. The Bad Stranger warning is a horrible one to have to give, just when your child is expanding into love and interest for the whole world. But you can't shirk it, and it would be madness to water it down too much. Some formulae for giving it are:

- 'Remember the wolf dressed up in grandmother's clothes? Well, unfortunately, there are some people a bit like that.

They seem friendly and look nice, but inside they are as bad as wolves. So don't talk to strangers, just in case.'

- 'Most people are friendly to children, and wouldn't harm them. But there are a few – who look just the same – who have got a sort of illness that makes them want to take children away from their parents and hurt them. So don't talk to strangers, just in case.'

You don't have to give a child nightmares by spelling out the atrocities which have happened to other children: the threat of 'being taken away' is quite terrifying enough to ram the message home. Additional points to stress are:

- Most people are good and kind BUT

- You can't judge by appearances.

- Mummy and Daddy would never send anyone to fetch you without telling the teachers or telling you, and doing something to prove it was the right person. This may be over-effective, but never mind. When I was eight I flatly refused to go home with someone from my father's office, although Reverend Mother and three other nuns knew it was OK and tried every tactic of persuasion they knew. I hid my small brothers behind me and stood my ground like Joan of Arc.

- Sometimes bad strangers might pretend to be your parents or teachers, when they are trying to drag you off. Nobody would blame you for rudeness if you ran away, screamed 'He's not my daddy!' or even bit them. Call out to the good strangers to help you. Policemen are safest: or lady shop-keepers, or traffic wardens.

- Sometimes people you know quite well, and who are usually very kind, might ask you to do strange things which you feel are wrong. You don't have to do them. You belong to yourself, not to anyone else. Even your parents.

- Bottoms and willies are private. Nothing wrong with them, they're just private. You don't have to pay any attention to anyone who wants to show you his willy or see yours, unless he's a doctor and your mummy or daddy are there.

It is a fine balance between encouraging friendliness and lack of prejudice, and safeguarding a child who is sometimes outside alone. Most of us err on the side of caution, but there is a real risk of painting the whole of the world outside the family as a nest of murderers, perverts and child-killers. The risk is partly that you may produce a fearful, mistrustful, xenophobic child: even if you don't mind that, bear in mind the equal danger that he might one day find out that *one* stranger is perfectly friendly. And not tell you, but quietly assume you were wrong about the rest, too.

9. Money Talks: But what does it say?

Amazingly early, children find out about money. Two-year-olds drop coins into slots crooning 'Munghymunghymunghy!' They know it is 'of value', not like pebbles in a bucket. These clinking discs are kept in special places, always put away, protected by zips and flaps: they are urgently sought for in shops, looked at with care, shut away in ringing tills. Munghy! It has an aura of power and mystery and carefulness. It is the tribal totem. Later on, they hear parents use the word anxiously, gleefully, gloomily: 'It's a lot of money . . . fine if you've got the money . . . did you bring any money?' It is a universal excuse for deprivations, absences, frustrations: 'Too much money . . . can't afford it . . . Daddy's got to go away to work, to earn money . . . Mummy does a job while you're at playgroup, to get money for nice things . . .'

Psychologists have traced children's awareness of money. First a child gets the principle of exchange: sweets for coins across the counter. Gradually he develops some idea of scale (can't buy a Ferrari for 40p). Then of divisibility (one small girl quoted in research didn't realize yet that you can still have a 10p lolly even if you've got 20p). Next comes the idea of earning (money for services), or circulation (Daddy gets money from his boss to give to the coalman), and finally such concepts as profit (shopkeepers charge more than they paid out) and value-adding (buy a stick and a cloth, make a puppet, make a profit). Finally he grasps interest and saving, and he is well on the way to credit cards, tax avoidance, Eurobond trading and a numbered bank account in Switzerland. So much for the nuts and bolts. The interest, and the problem, lies more in the emotional and moral aspects of money.

Somewhere, a child has got to find answers to the following questions and they will stay with him all his life. How do you

59

decide how much money different things are worth? Or how much different jobs are worth paying? Does paid work make people worth more? How much profit is it fair to make? When is it right to get into debt? Are rich people better than poor people? Or worse? Or neither? Why do some people have no money at all, and starve, while others waste it? What is the difference between being a saver and being a miser? The answers to all of these will be implicit in things you and other people say, in a child's hearing, in what you do and how you do it.

At any level of income, you can mess this one up. Poor-but-honest families can give the wrong messages every bit as much as rich-and-careless ones. I myself belong by nature to the frugal school of thought, and nurture a romantic idea that growing up in a poor family builds character. Part of me believes this, yet I never can forget George Orwell's devastating description of the Comstock family in *Keep the Aspidistra Flying*: they were poor and careful with money, and

> 'The first effect of all this was to give him a crawling reverence for money. In those days he actually hated his poverty-stricken relatives – his father and mother, Julia, everybody. He hated them for their dingy homes, their dowdiness, their joyless attitude to life, their endless worrying and groaning over threepences and sixpences. By far the commonest phrase in the Comstock household was "We can't afford it".'

The key word here is 'joyless'. Dozens of autobiographies record a different picture of growing up in a relatively poor family: of fun and laughter and enjoyment of the free pleasures of sunlight and moonlight and public parks; of children reading their way through the public libraries and building ingenious go-carts out of old prams. Children like these, brought up not to be defeated by poverty, are by far the best and happiest custodians of money when they do have it in later years. The ones who splurge and debauch, or turn mean and snobbish, are those whose parents have treated it as an obsessive and burdensome worry. You and I may know that money *is* an obsessive and burdensome worry: the trick is not to make the children old before their time.

The opposite peril is the over-monied household. How are you going to stop your child being inadvertently wounding, patronizing and otherwise nasty about his own plushy Christmas presents? How are you going to dissuade your daughter from swanking offensively about her My Little Pony Dream Wonderland Beauty Castle? On the whole, the amazing fact is that you don't have to do anything except shut up and not make things worse by trying too hard. Up to the age of about ten, unless they have been corrupted by a particularly materialistic family or school, children are hazy about monetary value. They won't be offensive about possessions unless you encourage them to be: there are very few children who don't have something to swank about. Be neutral. 'So Lisa hasn't got a Pony Castle? That's lucky that you have, it'd be boring if you had the same. Do you think she'll let you go round and see the trains rattle by her window again?' Avoid the emotive word 'poor' when talking about anyone you know: it conjures up visions of Little Match Girls and everyone sleeping in a hovel around the family pig. I have heard of children solemnly offering their pocket-money to the parents of friends who have been incautiously described as 'poor'. At least they got a first-hand experience of how strangely touchy adults are about this curious stuff, money.

On the other hand, there is nothing wrong with letting young children know about poverty farther afield. Television appeals are always met with a blaze of young generosity: passing on toys, raising money for Third World children and writing them letters are all sources of real and lasting joy and understanding.

The real problem comes when children ask, directly or implicitly, why some people are poor and others rich. Why isn't life fair? The temptation to give a trite answer is overwhelming: after all, it is one of the biggest and saddest mysteries in the world: the rich man in his castle, the poor man at his gate, and whether it was indeed God who set them high and lowly and ordered their estate. You can explain about famines and droughts and earthquakes; you can talk of 'luck', or try some basic monetarist economics (or Marxist theory, if that way inclined); you could even, though heaven forbid, try and stand up a shaky, but reassuring theory that good hardworking people never end up on the breadline.

But it is hard to do more than be honest about the unfairness, frank about the bafflement, and reiterate that money itself is neither a god nor a demon, but neutral. Some people deserve it and don't get it, others have it handed to them on a plate by inheritance. Some enjoy it, some let it ruin their lives. You can say that it doesn't matter, isn't everything, and can't buy you love: but on the other hand it would be madness not to teach children to respect it and save some up for a rainy day. Shake the kaleidoscope, make your own philosophical pattern, only don't leave anything out.

Pocket-Money is the first practical application of it. A curious aspect of this, in Britain at least, is that surveys show that the wealthier the family, the less pocket money the children tend to get. One TV personality gives her children, at eight years old, only 1p a day. In the homes of manual workers the children may get up to £2 a week.

I regard this with great cynicism. In the well-off household, the children get bought a great many things by their parents anyway. But it seems crazy to me to give a child only 7p a week, or even 10p. At present prices, he or she has no chance whatsoever of learning to handle money. It is not fair to make a child save up for two months for the price of an ice-lolly or a comic. Pay silly sums like that and you are encouraging the child to think of his money as different to yours – as a sort of toy. You exaggerate your power: if you buy a moderate toy for £7, you are underlining that an adult has a hundred times the spending power of a child, over and over again. The child feels powerless and aggrieved.

On the other hand, give a child £1 and he feels a sense of responsibility. He sees, dazzled, that if he didn't buy anything for a year, he could save for a whole electric car set. He makes decisions, he divides it up: he splurges 50p on a toy space monster, then learns the bitter feeling of wishing he hadn't; he puts the money in a savings account, and sees it visibly growing. He gives 25p to charity and is told that it has bought rice for a whole family in Ethiopia and put them two days further away from death by starvation. He gets a small taste of power and responsibility and the dilemmas of money. On the whole I favour giving pocket-money on the generous side if you can.

Earning is another useful concept. There are few legal openings for a child of seven to earn, but parental doses of pocket money can be earned or docked with great profit to all. I dock a few pence a time for swearing, spitting, hitting and such behaviour during the week, which encourages a grasp of subtraction; and I pay small sums for household jobs beyond the normal call of duty. (Beware: children can grow very mercenary around six, and start charging for table clearing and bedroom tidying. Don't be taken for a mug.) Earning one's first money is a great and solemn delight. Do not ruin it by indulgently giving your child double the agreed rate: the sense of really having *earned* five pence is better than the sense of being patronized with twenty.

Spending of one's own first money has to be free. Some families control it far too dictatorially. Obviously, really foul sweets or dangerous objects have to be controlled or banned, but otherwise it is a child's prerogative to waste his own money. The cold, hollow sense of having been cheated by a shoddy, over-packaged toy is something we all yearn to protect our children from, but we have no right to. In the catch-phrase of British politics when a Chancellor resigned, 'Advisers Advise and Ministers Decide.' Parents are only advisers, and it is hell. One of the most arduous task of middle motherhood is standing around for ages in toyshops while an anxious, half-miserly and half-yearning child peers at all the price labels and tries to make decisions. Grit your teeth. Take a paperback. Only don't take over.

Swopping I take an unconventional view. I do not think parents have much right to interfere with the curious inter-child commerce of these years. If your child is one of the sort who is prone to swop a £50 state-of-the-art supertoy for two marbles and a piece of chocolate, then let him. (Unless you are quite sure he has been bullied into it: speak to both children, if necessary.) If he actually wants the rubbish, then say goodbye to your money and learn your lesson: it is not fair to impose adult value-systems upon young children. If you really cannot bear seeing vital tools, like construction kits, leaving the house then say he can only swop things he has bought himself (not presents) without special permission.

Giving is a more difficult area. On the whole, for a quiet life and level relations with neighbours, a good rule is that children never take money from anyone outside the family without your knowing, and never give them any either – unless via a proper charity. Nor should children this age lend, or borrow: it too quickly becomes untrackable, out of control, and a source of resentment all round.

You may get it all entirely right. But I can tell you one difficulty that still might lie ahead. Teach a child to handle money sensibly, and you find yourself saddled with explaining that people who fall on hard times with no reserves are not necessarily (*pace* the right-wing theoreticians) feckless or stupid. One well-heeled child I knew stopped once in front of a tramp near Charing Cross and loudly asked her mother, 'Why didn't this man open a Young Saver Account when he was little?' Glares from dosser in cardboard box, a guilty fiver from Mummy failing to appease his dignity; and off fled Mummy and Young Saver down the Embankment, the sound of harassed explanations fading ineffectually on the chill evening air.

10. Hard Wearing: Cracking the dress code

Sometime between leaving off Babygros and being fitted for a wedding outfit, children develop a dress sense. The later it happens, frankly, the luckier you are. If you have a child who wishes to wear the same pattern of tattered unisex track suit, in ascending sizes, from the age of four to the age of consent, then your only problem is getting that child smartened up occasionally for a few hours. This may be an ordeal at the time (I well remember my own technique of going rigid and screaming when someone tried to force me into a red velvet party frock with lace collar) but it will save you money and, on balance, save you irritation too. Children look adorable in fancy clothes, but an overly clothes-conscious infant is a pain in the neck as well as a drain on the purse. Not only is there the logistical problem that whatever such a child fancies wearing at any given moment is either in the wash, too small, or costs £70; but a small child constantly preening herself in the mirror is not a seemly sight. A healthy, active, unselfconscious rag-bag is easier to live with. Most children fall between the two categories, not caring overmuch about anything except comfort, but enjoying brief crazes for certain favoured sweatshirts, or threadbare jumpers with pictures knitted into them.

Whichever temperament of child you have, it is obvious that in the three-to-eight age group the clothes business is substantially different to what it was before.

Run out and play Dear

Nappies are only a memory, sick-ups are rare, and most importantly of all, the child is beginning to become independent in
dressing. This precious independence (precious to you, I mean,
because you can get a cup of coffee drunk in peace in the
mornings) should be cherished and encouraged with easy slip-
on clothing, wide necks and elastic waists. Little boys look
wonderful in real shirts with cuff buttons, but the drawbacks
are obvious. Children at this mucky, active age need a lot of
clothes, often a daily change of everything including the sweater: there is room for perhaps one or two fidgety 'best' outfits
at most. What there is not room for, at their bewildering speed
of growth, is fashion. If you are wise, you will set your face
against it and never *ever* recommend anything to a child so
young on the grounds that it is 'trendy' or 'fashionable'. To
quote one harassed urban mother with a smart sultry moppet
in tow, 'Everything she has which isn't outgrown she says is
out of date, and vice versa.' Her daughter is six years old.
Fashion will, of course, influence what they wear because
fashion decrees what the chainstores carry: but to encourage it
wilfully is madness. It is also, in my admittedly slightly eccentric
view, madness to encourage little girls this age to be 'feminine'.
There will be time enough for that later on: for now let them
run and rip and swing unselfconsciously in boyish clothes. It
is, after all, a freedom many women fought to gain for them.

If you have been jogging along happily with handed-down baby
and toddler clothes until now, you should know that there are
clearly stratified levels in the lucrative children's clothes market,
and be aware of which kind of shop you have strayed into.
Here is a cynic's guide:

Top of the Tree Largely thanks to the fertility of the British
Royal Family, there has been a renaissance of very grand children's clothes. In any big city now there is somewhere selling
cream woollen coats with velvet collars, embroidered shirts in
fine cotton lawn, unwashable Fair Isle sweaters, and raw silk
ballgowns for little girls of four. The boys' shorts will be long,
with turn-ups; the shoes will be soft leather. Everything needs

ironing or steam-pressing with care, most things need dry-cleaning. They will break your heart. These clothes are designed for parents with nannies whose mission in life is to starch and wipe the children four times daily. They cost a lot, and their only advantage is that they can be handed down through the family (indelible stains permitting) for fifty years. It must also be said that those beautiful cloth coats with adult detail in the seaming are damned uncomfortable and stiff around five-year-old arms. I know, I used to wear one.

Très Très Trendy Whereas the shops above are targeted at Royals, pseudo-royals, social climbers and fogey sentimentalists, this lot is more likely to attract the new establishment: pop stars with accessory kids who are always being photographed in magazines, actresses with massive guilt complexes about being on tour for weeks, and party people who somehow think they will feel better about continuing their hedonistic lifestyle if their children, too, look vaguely as if they were on the way to Annabel's. The shops sell ra-ra skirts, layered Fifties petticoats, drainpipe jeans for boys which hardly go over their poor little ankles, multicoloured patchwork jackets from Bali, sequinned DJs for little boys, and every kind of tarty dancewear and impossible bodysuits for little girls. These clothes are expensive, but none of the designers will have taken much account of lingering toddler pot-bellies, washing machines, or the need to go to the lavatory in a hurry. They will snag, fade, run and rip in a week. But it doesn't matter because they will be out of fashion by then, and if you bought them you have more money than you need anyway.

Upmarket Many of these will come from Italy or America, and be beautifully made and designed and priced accordingly. They will be in classic styles with an original twist (like pink corduroy dungarees), cost a lot but wash beautifully, and be passed down through the family for years. If you buy them, buy them a shade too big or your heart will be broken the moment the child grows out of the garment. Actually, the most trouble-free way to enjoy really good quality children's clothes is to have an affluent and good-natured neighbour with an only child a year older than yours and immaculate taste. For several years my daughter was thus equipped with wonderful clothes: comfortable, beautiful and easy to look after. Then she grew six inches and outstripped the older child. Curses.

Whereas only caprice is likely to make the ordinary mother buy from the first two kinds of shop, this expensive category is worth considering occasionally, especially with a big family or a collection of nephews and nieces to pass on to. Many of the clothes are so good they can be sold on if you are broke.

Chainstore Probably the mainstay for most of us. Track-suits, T-shirts, sweatshirts (preferably without advertisements for naff toys all over them), trousers with elastic backs so lazy boys don't have to use the button and zip, T-shirt dresses for little girls which pull on easily over the head, six-packs of knickers and socks – these are the essentials of the working wardrobe. And children ought, on the whole, to be thought of as manual workers: their clothes should be tough and cheerful and forgettable. We are, in the West, well served by chainstores. The only irritations are the creeping sloganization of clothes (why should an innocent five-year-old want to walk around labelled Surf City, or Cool Dude?) and the utter failure of chainstores to understand that children grow at unpredictable rates. They still assume that if you want cold-weather clothes you will stock up on them in September, so by January (when it really gets cold) their shelves will contain nothing but spring dresses and Hawaiian shirts.

Mail Order In Britain, Clothkits is king. But there are others, too, and for country-dwellers and working mothers they are a boon and a delight. Admittedly, every other middle-class child in your locality will probably be wearing the same jolly print skirt and kangaroo-knit sweater at times, but that is a small price to pay for something reasonably priced, high quality, and not involving parking a car in a town and trudging round shops. Most children don't much enjoy clothes shopping anyway, so you might as well measure them and send off. The order forms, however, are cleverly designed to make you spend more than you meant to.

Downmarket Most supermarket chains have a children's clothes section, and this is one of the main homes of the really downmarket clothes. These are, by and large, grim: hastily sewn clothes in cheap man-made fabrics look all right for a wash or two, then begin to show their low origins. However, they are all that many of us can afford at times, especially when children are growing very fast: you should approach anything cheap, though, with great cynicism and give the sleeves sharp, unforgiving tugs in the shop. Often you can get far better value at:

Jumble and Second-hand Sales In affluent districts of big cities, the most amazing clothes (often from the Royal-ish shops) turn up as jumble or in 'opportunity shops'. No parent on earth should be ashamed of using them. Rose's best beloved party dress for three years cost me £1; I snapped up some wonderful shorts and T-shirts one summer for 50p the lot, pure cotton and nicely styled.

Home-made Best value of all. One cautionary tale, though: a girl I know set out to make a fleecy track suit, spent three hours and £8 on fabric, and then saw a virtually identical one for £6 in an upmarket shop sale. Virtue is not always rewarded, after all.

11. Heavy Petting: Terrible gerbils and gangland goldfish

There is, no doubt about it, some special relationship between children and animals. Watch a child pat a horse, or pick up a complaisant kitten, and you know it. Observe an even smaller child, colouring in the white patches on the family dog, or a toddling baby using the family Labrador as a walking frame. Grown men wax sentimental at the memory of a childhood cat, and I myself carried a curl of bull-mastiff hair in my locket through all the traumas of adolescence. (I was forever having to open the locket and turf out the ginger, black or mousey hair of swains who didn't come up to the mark. But the wiry curl of sand-coloured dog hair stayed inviolate.) Furthermore, when asked to write about a 'sacred early memory' for some charity book, I found the typewriter mysteriously producing data I had not consciously examined for years: the story of Birdie the cage bird whose remarkable life spanned years of my childhood. Oh yes, animals matter to children.

A cool and unsentimental look at the whole subject is required, however, or you will end up with a bitten child or a bored one; or at best with a psychopathic cat, a ruined carpet and a tankful of dead goldfish.

If you are already a confirmed pet-lover you don't much need this chapter. Except for one heavy warning which everyone needs: existing pets, however sweet, may deeply resent a child. Dogs are especially jealous: never, ever leave them alone with a small child until you are more than sure of their benevolence. Remember that a dog which didn't mind a baby, or a comparatively slow-moving toddler, may get edgier as the child gets older. It is rare – usually it works the other way – but it happens. The same goes for other people's dogs when you are visiting: a child's face is placed too low to risk even a brief bad-tempered snap. And beware of cats' claws. Most cats will do anything to avoid confrontation, but if grabbed by the tail they will panic in a big way. Make children treat them with all the deference that you do, and hammer home the message that just as they themselves don't have to kiss and hug anyone they don't want to (modern anti-child-abuse message No. 1 – as taught in all good schools), cats don't have to, either.

I have the right not to be kissed or stroked if I don't want to

If you've never had much to do with animals, but feel your child would benefit from one, here is a beginners' guide. I have made it as depressing as possible, purposely to counteract the cuddly, furry, sweet-eyed trusting appeal of the animals which are trying to get in and live with you. I speak as one who has a kitten on my shoulder, another one eating my left shoe, a pig snorting outside the window and a moribund baby hedgehog stretched out by the kitchen stove.

Dogs Everyone knows their good points: one forgives them a lot because they are so sickeningly devoted and uncritical. But until a child is over ten, and capable (depending on your neighbourhood) of exercising a dog herself, it is madness to buy one unless you want one for your own, parental, sakes. Dogs need a lot of rather expensive food, daily exercise and regular worming, especially if children are around. The *Toxicara canis* worm is a serious menace which can cause blindness. Also, in many areas you will quite rightly be expected to clear up the dog's messes yourself. Carrying little white spades and plastic bags around is not everyone's idea of spontaneous enjoyment of the natural world.

If you do get a dog, pay attention to the breed. Big ones are often, oddly enough, better-natured then small 'toy' dogs, and it is a truism that mongrels are nearly always more pleasant than thoroughbreds. Show dogs have been bred entirely for appearance, and not temperament, so a vicious, untrustworthy bitch will be allowed to breed if she is beautiful enough. Mongrels, on the other hand, are bred for company or else by accident: the result is calmer and friendlier.

But if you really are a dog beginner, don't just ask one person's advice, ask several. And get it trained: go to obedience classes and be barked at by a fierce, tweedy, lady dog-trainer. Dog-training classes are a terrible bore to non-enthusiasts, but undisciplined and untrained dogs are a dangerous nuisance. Talking of which, do not, absolutely not, be tempted to buy a sweet-looking, big-headed puppy from one of the 'attack' breeds: Rottweilers, Dobermanns, even Alsatians have an appalling record of turning on children without warning. Sometimes they kill them. In seconds.

Cats are independent, cussed animals. They can be very frustrating for children because they insist on choosing for themselves whose knee they sit on, and they prefer people who don't move around all the time. If you get kittens, choose the boldest and brashest of the litter. Two will be more amusing than one, because they wrestle and pounce and buoy up one another's confidence in the face of big looming children. House cats need no exercising, but flit in and out of the catflap: however, if you insist on keeping one in a flat, you must bravely face up to the question of cat litter. Litter trays, as used by adult cats, are Not Nice. They are especially Not Nice if you have a crawling baby or are pregnant yourself (they are a disease risk to pregnant women). Litter costs a lot. So does catfood.

On the other hand, small children can get a real relationship going with cats. Nicholas and Rose used to go carol-singing to our late cat Nelson at Christmas, saying, 'If you had a mince pie or some money, you'd give it us, wouldn't you, Nellie?'

Rabbits and Guinea-Pigs are small, portable, furry and vegetarian (therefore, their droppings are not too nasty). They can live outdoors in hutches, so you don't have the smell in the kitchen. What could be nicer? Well, it would be nicer not to feel so guilty. They are transparently, chronically bored in hutches. They want to run on the grass. So you make a run, and the next-door dog jumps in and kills them. Or they tunnel out and you have to spend hours crawling round the hedge because they might die if they spent the night out.

They also – and here is the crunch – need daily handling to keep them tame enough for children, and both species scrabble in your hands, which alarms shy children and makes them drop (and possibly injure) the animal. After the first rapturous week a child will grow tired of them anyway, so you have to tame and handle them yourself. It is necessary to read a few leaflets about these animals, as there are all sorts of strange rules one might not know about: did you know that guinea-pigs need daily vitamin C? That Dutch Miniature rabbits mustn't overdose on lettuce? Is there really room in your mind for these facts?

Having said all that, it is possible for a family with a garden to get a rabbit, let it hop round the kitchen from babyhood, totally tame it, then let it live out of doors. I know one family with a hand-reared tame rabbit in the garden. It has brought in, and tamed in turn, a succession of wild ones. The family play and garden surrounded by friendly, strokeable bunnies. It is an idyll. Sheridan did it, and good for her: but I didn't manage it; and only you can judge whether you would.

Guinea-pigs can never live free for long, and have, frankly, the most boring temperament of any animal I know.

Gerbils and Hamsters Even smaller and more portable, and they inspire less guilt because at least they have a wheel to go round in. But gerbils in particular have to live indoors. Do you have a corner where the cage won't get knocked over or trodden on? Do you have children who will keep it clean, and the water changed?

As far as children are concerned, these small rodents are better winter entertainment than rabbits because they are always visible. However, they are frail creatures and die more readily, which is harrowing.

It is certainly fun for children to handle these little animals;

but they do tend to let them go, and then you have to get them back from under the wardrobe. The same goes for mice, except that in my experience once a mouse gets away it stays away. Sometimes it mates with your own wild mice and you get intriguing piebald pests going through your larder for years afterwards, and you don't feel like poisoning them because you are, in a sense, their granny.

Rats put a lot of mothers off. But they have all the good qualities of the group above, and a lot more intelligence. You can teach a rat tricks, at least. Still, I wouldn't recommend them wholeheartedly for under-tens.

Fish Don't buy goldfish or tropical fish, however much your child pleads, unless you actually like the idea of a handsome tankful in the house. A lone, sad goldfish in an unfiltered and unoxygenated bowl is a miserable sight after a while. It is also a bad example to your child of care for living creatures. So you have to fling yourself into the business of getting a proper bubbling machine and a big tank and giving them plants to swim around. The trouble is that a young child may well lose interest half-way through this process.

We bought fish because the children begged for them, and developed a curious problem. All the fish died, except Albert. Every time we put more fish in with Albert, they died too. Albert flourished. We decided he either had a form of fishy AIDS, or was a murderer. So we spent a whole year with one lonely, murderous fish alone in a vast tank, wasting electricity and light. In the end we put him in the garden pond to sink or swim. He lived there until the great drought of 1989, when one must assume he perished. The children had forgotten him by then, so we were at least spared the carpentry of making an Albert Memorial.

Birds The guilt problem arises again. Nobody has ever established that birds don't mind being in cages. I think they do. I suppose if the cage is big enough and hangs in a window, and the bird has plenty of millet and a bell and a piece of cuttlefish and music on the radio to sing along with, it isn't too bad a life. Check that you are not buying a species which ought to be protected (like the African finch). Children will enjoy the bird, in a half-hearted sort of way.

Ponies Unless you are horsey yourself, think very, very carefully. Neglected backyard ponies are now a serious problem in Britain. A pony means feed, stabling, tack, shoeing (more expensive than shoeing an extra child), and unexpected vet's bills. Only a dedicated riding child, who has proved his or her keenness, should be given a pony. If it has not got a decent-sized paddock, it will need exercise every single day. Even when it is proved to be nothing but a liability, the child will be fond enough of it to make a dreadful fuss when you sell a pony or pass it on.

Farm Animals Penelope Leach has pointed out that six months of hand-rearing a lamb or calf is more educational and memorable for a child than a lifetime of cleaning out rabbit cages. However, this option is not open to you if you live in a third-floor flat in town. Also, adults have to be really clued-up and dedicated to manage farm animals, especially since a half-grown sheep which wants to sit on your knee is a problem in anyone's terms. It may be better to opt for visits to a farm park or a City Farm. But I live in a glass house, so shouldn't throw stones at anyone who falls for the farm option. The piglets are due any day now, thank you.

On balance, pets are worth it. They teach children gentleness and respect for living things. They are pleasant, uncritical companions in a world peopled by figures of authority and, with their short life-cycles, they provide a good way to learn about death. Too often, television and games and Hallowe'en grotesqueries portray death as violent and gory: a child who gets the chance to bury a pet rabbit and make it a wooden cross, or stroke a dead cat for the last time and feel it as lifeless as plasticine beneath the fur, is getting a clearer, calmer idea. One day in January we watched together over a sick orphan lamb slipping peacefully into its last sleep by the fire. It was sad, but there was a reality about it which we were glad, in the end, to share with the children.

Although – did you guess? – it was barely a week before the next one turned up.

12. Toys: Junk and joyfulness

I saved up writing this chapter, deliberately, until our family was half-way through moving house. I wanted to speak to you from a position of authority, that is, standing knee-deep in broken plastic legs, defunct spaceships, squashed crayons, dollies' fridges with the doors hanging off, half-finished model windmills, legless Lego-men and gappy jigsaws.

And so I am. I feel, as most parents feel, rather nauseous at the sight of it all. Look at it, the toy box of any moderately prosperous household: so many bygone treats, thrilling presents, guilt offerings, surprises from Santa and pocket-money treasures lie around us, reduced to a sea of unwanted plastic. We feel guilty of environmental vandalism. We fear we have spoiled our children, and resent the sense of having given in to a massive commercial confidence trick. At this moment, I am surrounded by bin bags, jumbled boxes and tea chests, while both children are upstairs playing rapturously with a set of model shops which I made – rather sketchily – out of matchboxes during a rare fit of creativity three years ago. At such moments it is tempting to say that all the rest was pointless.

But it wasn't. The truth is more complicated, and all this resentment only obscures the real issues. The subject of toys is very difficult to disentangle from other dangerously emotional aspects of parenthood. Toys point up our fear of spoiling children, for one thing; for another, they play on our educational hang-ups and our deep unadmitted aspirations. We all desire children to live up to certain intellectual and personal standards: see the disgust on a scholarly father's face as his son fires off plastic jellies from his Ghostbuster gun, or the feminist mother's discomfiture at the sight of her little girl lovingly putting a nylon frilled wedding dress on to an orange rubber pony with a lurex mane. There is plenty of harmless merriment to be got from watching a tasteful upper-middle-class household at Christmas time: here is the Liberty-decorated Christmas Tree, here are the impeccably restrained Swedish baubles and the Habitat crackers. And here, beneath the tree, waiting to assault the parents' delicate sensibilities, are a My Little Pony Dream Beauty Parlour in appalling colours and tacky fabric, a Sindy doll in bondage leatherwear, and a gruesome reproduction Kalashnikov machine-gun. Poor parents: torn between sense and taste and a praiseworthy desire to let children choose for themselves, they gave in. No wonder they are drinking so much wine. It is depressing to buy all your nursery fabrics from Colefax & Fowler, only to have garish Care Bears plonked down on them.

The toy industry is, quite frankly, rather a revolting one: at least in its internationalist aspects, and where it deals with the over-fours. Younger children's toys are not too bad: by law, they are strong and safe, and many are extremely well designed: a Fisher-Price farm, or Tomy push-and-go toy, will last out your children's time and sponge down beautifully for the playgroup jumble sale. Also, toddlers are not style victims. They really don't care whether it is the model-before-last they are playing with.

However, the world of toys for older children is a none-too-pleasant jungle. If you want to know how these people, the manufacturers and marketers, really think then visit a commercial toy fair: listen to them talking about 98 per cent market saturation targets and 'aggressive marketing'; see them drool at the thought of 'tying-in' with a television cartoon, or getting a celebrity to 'write' a range of bland little books about some cynically, deliberately designed merchandising character. You cannot separate toys from books and television in this area: when it comes to pallid, bland creations like the Shoe People or Victoria Plum, it is painfully obvious that a shrewd commercial mind has designed the duvet-covers and pencil boxes with far more attention than ever went into writing the books.

Toy manufacturers have a strong commercial interest in colonizing our children's minds. They push 'collectable' ranges, hoping to addict them: you must have *all* the Ghostbusters, all the Transformers, all the clothes and accessories for Barbie or

79

Sindy. Toyshops, even some of the most famous, tend to go along with this because it is more convenient to have predictably packaged and well-established ranges on your shelves than to scan all the catalogues, chat up independent, quirky manufacturers and carry an original range. As a result, it is possible to walk round some of the biggest toyshops in the Western world and not find a simple child's drum or set of wooden bricks. A spokesman for Hamleys in London once told me: 'We are governed by what people want, and I suppose they are governed to a considerable extent by what is on television, or advertised strongly on television. Some of them are tacky, horrible things but they just do sell. We try to carry handmade toys, wooden toys, but you know how it is . . .' I do, I do. But personally I now spend rather more money at shops like Tridias of Bath (and mail order) where Charlotte and Robin Cook have a firm rule that 'If everyone else has got it, we won't bother.' They have an extraordinary range of toys from all over the world, but without the pretentiously snobbish anti-plastic attitude of some other independent toyshops. Indeed, one of the most successful battery toys we ever had was their Inter-Galactic Missile-Firing Chicken, a lifesize plastic rooster which strides across the carpet, flaps its wings and shoots off plastic missiles in all directions. 'We found it at a foreign toy fair, and it seemed to be the ultimate answer to the problem of aggressive war toys.' It certainly is: it is a fat yellow chicken, but can outshoot anything from the nursery NATO arsenal and send itself up rotten at the same time. Anyone who gets depressed with grey and khaki plastic tanks and little children nursing rocket-launchers needs a Missile-Firing Chicken to cheer them up. That one is definitely going in the tea chest, and coming with us to the new house.

But here ends the sermon. Among the tatty dross, there are treasures, whose value is in the eye of the small beholder. Even some constituents of the most offensively oversold ranges of toys are actually very well-made. Children are also rather well-made, and have a great inborn capacity to mix the toys together, break the manufacturers' rules and play precisely what games they want to. I once got home to find several hideously macho, muscle-bound plastic figurines lying in a frilly doll's cradle being nursed by a teddy bear and a rag doll. 'They're poorly,' I was told. 'They're being made better. Then they'll have a holiday on the beach.' Considering that the patients were all still wearing their ammunition belts and SAS scowls, I thought it a most commendable leap of the imagination into a more peaceful world than the designers would have liked. (And no, it wasn't a girl speaking. Boys need dolls too: why else do you think the toy soldier was developed?) After that, I gave up my vain attempts to ban guns and war toys, and was rewarded by the spectacle of the tank being used as a tractor, to pull a toy plough, and by a gradual decline of interest in guns except during certain brief, vicious, all-boy interludes with particularly hawkish visitors.

There are three useful principles to use in managing toys. The first thing is, periodically to *put things away*. Any set of toys becomes boring: rather than keep buying new ones, rotate them. The second is to have periodical blitzes (just before birthdays and Christmas are good times) in which you, as the Managing Director of this household, firmly reassemble all the sets into different boxes, getting construction sets and play-people and doll's house things and soldiers from the fort sorted out. Cross-fertilization is a good thing in play, but can end up in sordid chaos out of which no decent creative game could ever emerge. By seven, children will begin to be able to do this job themselves, but it is too daunting beforehand. If, like ours, your children clearly have too many toys, this is the time to Put Away or – even better – Give Away.

The second principle is *try not to buy things too early*. Just because you always longed for an electric train set is no reason to give one to a cack-handed five-year-old who won't be able to fit the trains on to the rails properly. Just because you remember the joy you got from your John Bull printing set, don't foist a lot of fiddly rubber bits on a child who can barely spell out CAT. If a child gets given a toy for which it clearly is not ready, then *put it away*, almost immediately. Otherwise it will be dispersed and ruined before the time is ripe to use it constructively. Also, don't give presents so lavish that they only baffle the child. There is a terrible temptation to do this, especially if you are rather well-off and guilty about being out at work. The child's capacity for awed wonder is something so marvellous to adults that we sometimes – selfishly – try to jack it up for our own pleasure. If this five-year-old is so delighted at finding a dewy cobweb in the garden, we reason erroneously, just think what he will say when we give him a scaled-down Lamborghini Countach with Briggs & Stratton four-stroke petrol engine and working gearbox! If he is so thrilled with his teddy bear, just imagine what he will say when he finds a fifteen-foot tall furry giraffe with light-up eyes peering into his bedroom! This way madness lies, for both of you. Fortunately, most of us cannot afford this particular form of child abuse.

The final – and most important – thing is to remember, especially when you begin to panic about spoiling a child, that there are two types of toys (irrespective of quality or longevity). Some are tools, and some are luxuries. The tools are obvious if

it's called "My Little Chainsaw" and it comes in powder blue with matching accessories

you look what you gave them at a younger age: you would not deny a baby his rattles or a toddler his bricks. If you couldn't get them, you would make them. In the same way, growing children need certain types of play for their mental and manual development. Never feel guilty about buying a really good construction set (even if it doesn't get used often at first); or a jigsaw, or a set of basic plastic play people, or drawing and painting equipment; remember that children actually need things with wheels, things that float, things that contain other things or tessellate with them to make patterns. They don't have to be over-elaborate or expensive, but it helps to keep it clear in your mind that you are buying the basic tools of his trade. He is a professional developer of his own mind and body. So it is not the same thing as lavishing all the latest Ghostbusters on a child, or indeed pandering to your own sentimental memories with handmade jack-in-the-boxes: these are luxuries.

The best advice on actual toys that I can offer takes the form of two lists. The first of things that you will never regret buying, although you do not by a long stretch need them all; and the second list comprises things that you probably *will* regret, bitterly, if you get them for this age group.

You will never regret:

- Ample, simple, drawing and painting equipment. Basic colouring books.

- Decent construction systems. Lego for architecture perhaps. Meccano or Brio Mec or Fischer-Technik for old-fashioned mechanical engineering. Lego Technik or Capsela for modern versions and the working of gears and motors. Only make your mind up early: don't buy a starter set of everything on the market.

- Some truly excellent series of figures and small accessories, such as Playmobil. The important thing about them is that they are just detailed enough to excite a sophisticated six-year-old, but not so 'finished' that there is nothing left to imagine. These series tend to come in small units, but are not oversold as 'collectable' – each box is a worthwhile toy in its own right.

- Balls. It is amazing how some families seem to have every kind of climbing frame and elaborate outdoor toy, but no football in sight. Perhaps a ball would merely underline the fact that they don't give their child enough playmates, adult or child.

- Kites. Simple ones, preferably cloth. Controllables come later.

- Good board games, which you and they actually play.

- Good children's tools. Carefully designed saws, hammers, planes, and so on, if kept in a separate place from other toys and used under discreet supervision, are a better guarantee of future safety than a mere hysterical ban on all sharp blades.

- Jigsaws of the right level, which can be hugely variable. Ignore the age group on the box – it will only upset you.

- A basic doll's house for which furniture can be bought or made in stages.

- A fort with soldiers. Call it history, if you must.

- A toy theatre. *But* for heaven's sake don't get carried away with frustrating tangly puppets. There is an East German type where the head is supported on a wire, with just two strings for the arms. This is as complicated as you should get before the child is ten. Believe me.

- Glove puppets and finger puppets.

- Dolls that your child actually wants and loves and chooses herself (or himself, come to that).

- Very good quality 'sets' that you couldn't possibly have assembled yourself: shape-printing sets, junior embroidery frames, a basic safe chemistry set perhaps, a pinhole camera kit.

- Peculiar, offbeat science kits that don't cost much: the cardboard models you build and power with a solar cell, the clock which runs off a potato, and so on. But for most science learning, alas, there is no substitute for the patient parent and a good children's book. Nothing is more irritating than to buy an impressive box marked 'make your own weather station', only to be ordered to get a jam jar and a balloon and a straw to make a barometer, something every boy scout ought to have known anyway.

- Very cheap, rather silly, possibly short-lived, but highly amusing novelties: magic tricks from China, East German wooden oddities, tiny torches with a spray of optic fibres coming out of them making sparkly patterns with their tips. I look out for them all year, and keep a stockpile in the attic for party bags and to help out Santa.

- Stuffed toys with pleasant expressions on their faces.

Just scraping, by the skin of its teeth, into this list is:

- A decent computer (for a child not younger than seven, I would say, but I am an old-fashioned bigot). It should be capable of taking the same type of programme they use at school, and of word processing as well as playing daft games (try the games out yourself: if they are too violent, be brave and ban them). There have been some scare stories recently about children becoming withdrawn, antisocial 'computer addicts': what this boils down to is that some parents are so timid, so fearful and unconfident about their own judgment that they allow children of seven to spend a great number of hours – sometimes forty a week in term-time – sitting alone in their bedrooms with nothing but a screen to play with, and don't remonstrate until the habit has been established for months. If a child spent that much time *reading* and had no friends, most of us would do something about it.

You will regret buying:

- Silly little paintboxes, with brushes whose bristles fall out the first time you wash them. Also felt pens (only rare children put the tops back on each time, and they dry up). Also very expensive and beautiful crayons like oil pastels which the child squashes and loses. If you can afford such luxuries, it is nice to give children good colours instead of garish crayon colours, but there is a middle way. Conté crayons are excellent.

- Anything made of the kind of thin plastic that breaks and produces jagged lethal edges.

- Anything whose only appeal is that it belongs to a set of merchandised figures, heavily advertised on television. If it has other merits, which are obvious (solidity for one), you won't regret it so much.

- Brand-new nine-day-wonder, outdoor toys. If your child wants to skateboard, either get her sessions on a friend's board for some weeks, or else get a decent second-hand one until you find out if she *really* wants to. The same with rollerskates, pogo sticks, and those curious bouncing platforms with balls in the middle. It even applies to bicycles.

- Superior kites that only Daddy understands and, even so, they get him into an awful temper.

- Gimmicky board games whose rules only Mummy understands, ditto. Also overtly 'educational' games which none of you will really ever touch.

- Anything that you buy out of guilt because their Maths/

Spelling/Reading doesn't seem to be good enough, and the packet promises it will teach them. It probably won't.

- Overcomplicated jigsaws. But you can always do them instead.

- Doll's houses fully equipped with everything the heart could desire, leaving no room or imagination and driving you mad when the bits get dispersed because the cheapest bit cost £10.50.

- Vast railway layouts, again leaving nothing for the child to invent, yearn for, and collect personally.

- Elaborate dolls your child hates the sight of. Also simple dolls, ditto: but at least you haven't wasted much money.

- Con-trick 'sets' which don't list the contents on the box, can't be inspected open in the toyshop, and prove to consist largely of printed instructions and over-priced bits of plastic moulding. They are much liked by the academically minded but bone-idle parent who thinks that by getting a 'Young Electrician' set he is somehow putting his child on the road to being the new Clive Sinclair. You can do better for a quarter the price at a good model shop with a sympathetic assistant.

- Computerized toys which only do one thing – such as testing spelling, or sums, or talking back to you in a harsh grating American voice.

- Remote control aeroplanes. They will fly away and not come back, because your child is much too young for them. Remote control cars at least don't get so far, so fast, but are rarely a favourite toy for more than a week.

- Stuffed toys with unpleasant leers on their faces.

The first list may sound expensive: but some of the things can be made, and some can be saved for. And the second is, in fact, very nearly as expensive. A few well-chosen toys, supplemented by coloured pebbles, are a better foundation for life than a sterile nurseryful of luxurious nothings. And it is worth putting some thought into the business of toys, because they are – at their best – agents of joy and fascination and growth of the spirit. And at their worst, bringers only of disappointment, cynicism, dust and ashes. They matter.

13. The Good Granny Guide

What does the word *grandmother* conjure up, for you? A sweet grey-haired old lady rocking quietly in her corner, or a slinky blonde of 43-going-on–15 with a tousled perm and the kind of energy that makes an exhausted new mother feel a hundred years old? And what is a granny for? Is she there to croon old folk tunes to your child, passing on the wisdom of generations and the tranquillity of age, or is her role to perch on the sofa drinking gin and explaining what you are doing wrong? Should she knit? Need she sniff so loudly at your sloppy housework?

The whole business of grandparenthood is increasingly confusing. A hundred years ago, in the days when people were unimaginably old at fifty, the generations were more distinct: families lived closer together, and the grandparental role was obvious. Today, families hardly ever live together as three generations for long, and with better health and longer life there can be extraordinary variations in age. All it takes is for a mother and daughter both to have babies in their teens or early twenties, and you can end up with a startlingly glamorous granny of forty-something, hitting the peak of her activities just as her daughter declines into the tearful muddle of early motherhood. 'Must dash, dear – I've got a meeting of the bench, then back to the boutique, then dress for the theatre tonight. Hope you find a baby-sitter in the end – ooza pretty baby den? Ciao, darlings!'

You can call me Grannikins

On the other hand, when both generations of women marry late and have babies in their thirties and forties, you get the opposite: a woman who is pushing seventy when she holds her first grandchild, and who may well bring a curious, inflexible set of Truby King attitudes with her all the way from the bracing 1940s. 'You shouldn't pick him up when he cries. You're making a rod for your own back, dear. Strict four-hourly feeding is healthiest. You'll overstimulate him with all that cuddling. Why haven't you got a nice, coach-built pram instead of that flimsy buggy? Don't hold him upright, you'll strain his back.'

Of course, there are gallant exceptions. There are brisk evergreen grannies who take over children for whole fortnights. There are cosy old bodies who never criticize but provide rocklike security for mother and child alike; and there are grandfathers who let little ones play by their workbench or waggle the tiller of their boat, hour after patient hour. Family life at its best is a self-renewing idyll, with happiness and good sense passing down the generations. Never mind what it is like at its worst: optimism is the keynote. However, in the interest of family harmony and a gentle release of steam, here is the official Good Granny Guide:

Mk I: Poor Old Granny She may be only sixty-two, but has decided to retire from the more strenuous side of life. Delighted though she is with the presence of a new or growing grandchild, changing nappies is quite out of the question. So are baths, floor-level romps, lifting, or learning to cope with those newfangled OshKosh dungaree fastenings.

She may well have driven you out of your mind during the first three hectic years, when most of the jobs of child-rearing are practical ones, but take heart. With her almost uncanny talent for sitting absolutely still and letting people bring her things, she will provide a useful focus for busy children. Above all, she should prove madly useful as an audience for those who wish to perform incomprehensible plays with a toy theatre, do a fairy dance over and over again, demonstrate somersaults or tell a very, very long and boring story about what teacher said in school.

Mk II: Retro-Granny She wants to help. Well, no, what she actually wants to do is to re-live every moment of her own enchanted motherhood, all those years ago. Your baby is *her* baby all over again, every line of its pudgy little face painfully, ecstatically reminiscent of her own darling's. Therefore it follows that if you fail to use the identical brand of zinc and castor-oil cream, the same gigantic pram and the precise type of kite-folded nappy and soggy woollen leggings as she did, you are cruelly betraying the family. Backpacks, slings, track suits and Velcro-fastened shoes will be greeted with shrill cries of alarm.

The only cure for this is to smile a lot and do your own thing. And remember that in thirty years' time, you will probably be driving your daughter mad with critiques of her solar-powered hovering pushchair and self-destruct nuclear nappies. It would be kind to pander to Retro-Granny with, at the very least, a few pairs of long grey shorts for boys and a bit of smocking for girls.

Mk III: Scatty Granny She is not at all sure about this business of grandmotherhood. Nobody down at the singles club could believe it when she told them. She can't remember a thing about children, because she was such a child herself when she had you: so she brazens it out with a lot of giggling and tickling. In fact, she fills more of the functions of a bachelor uncle or aunt than of a granny. Just pick up after her, sigh, and remember that children adore feckless adults. And be prepared for her to display a certain degree of alarm when her granddaughter starts looking too grown-up for comfort.

Mk IV: Dodgy Granny A few – very few – middle-aged people have so utterly forgotten their own years of motherhood that they are frankly not safe around babies. They drop fag ash in the carrycot, administer scalding hot drinks, refuse to believe that a bit of healthy dog dirt could harm anybody, and watch the telly instead of the moving toddler. Alas, in the early years you must be realistic and prudent without being overfussy: better an offended in-law than an injured child. But as your own children grow into the older age range, Dodgy Granny can become quite a good friend. It is possible to intimate, tactfully, to a six-year-old that Granny is a bit forgetful about safety, so needs help. She is not one to call in an emergency.

Mk V: Hostile Granny-in-law You were not good enough to marry her son (or daughter). You can tell this by the way she always addresses the child as 'poor little poppet'. On no account try to prove to her that you are a good mother/father. That way lies madness, because she won't have it. Just encourage her disapproving devotion, because it could lead to faultless baby-sitting: she will be keen to prove she is better than you, and will never mind how late you are back because it will simply prove her point. Call her in any time you feel the children need a bit of starching.

Mk VI: Stern Granny One of these once greeted her own daughter's fourth pregnancy with the words, 'I can't think why you're having another, dear, since the ones you've got don't seem to be under any proper control or discipline whatsoever.' Investigate her more closely: it may turn out that she went in for twenty-four-hour nannies and housekeepers, and boarding school at seven, in which case you can subtly let her know that you are well aware of the fact. But if she is a genuine martinet, prepared to administer reproofs and withhold pudding from small people who commit crimes like putting their elbows on the table, you should look on the bright side. Either the children will adore her and incidentally pick up some wonderful manners or, failing that, she will come in very handy as a threat.

Mk VII: Spoiling Granny 'Isn't Mummy strict with 'oo, poppet? Aaaah, it seems a shame. They're only young once. Come on, sweetums, let Granny buy you the sweety-weeties. Oh, aren't they the right kind? No, no throwums, my poppet! Ooops! Aaaah, never mind. Granny will pay for the broken bottles on the silly old shelf. Let Granny find you a little treat . . .'

Spoiling Granny is bearable as long as she is prepared to take the consequences. The crunch comes when she fails to pull up a wild child until he or she becomes really appalling – rude, ungrateful, foul-mouthed and thoroughly nasty in her house – and then she hands it over with pursed lips and mutterings about 'bad blood coming into the family'. No known cure.

Mk VIII: Perfect Granny She cooks wonderful meals, is never cross, cuts out dollies' clothes by the hour, tells wonderful stories of the old days, reads for hours and can do everything much better than you can. Babies go to sleep in her arms instantly, bigger children never give her a moment's trouble. With luck, she also remembers to keep saying what a super mother you are and how well-reared are your children. If she forgets this little detail, you may well feel inclined to jump off the nearest bridge.

But, all in all, grannies are a Good Thing. God bless them. Also bless grandfathers, who curiously seem less prone to fall into the above categories, having a healthy helping of male selfishness and *laissez-faire* to keep them nicely detached. One day, God willing, our own baby will produce a baby and we will be struck with awe at the sheer miraculousness of it, the continuing chain of creation springing from our own fast-fading flesh. The joy of it all may well make us a bit peculiar, in our turn. Meanwhile we are grateful for small blessings. No, honestly, we are. Really grateful. It must have taken hours to make, and it's a beautiful colour. What is it? A ballet cardigan? Marvellous . . . yes, she is a bit of a tomboy. Do her good, a peach cross-over cardigan . . .

14. Faith, Fears and Legends

One of the unexpected pleasures of parenthood is the conversation. Granted, there are moments of pure torment, when inquiring minds come padding through to your bedroom at 5.30 a.m. with a query about how old the sky is; but on the whole, talking to small children is good fun. Whoever would have thought, gazing at that scrunched-up little pink creature in the maternity ward, that you would get barely four years' start to prepare an answer to every mystery of the universe? Why is the night dark? What are those doggies doing? Where do babies come from? What is a Pry Minister and why do we have to do what she says? Do guinea-pigs go to heaven? What is far more awesome is the reflection that whatever you tell them, they will believe; and whatever they learn later on to prove you wrong, some tiny corner of the mind will retain that first, indelible lesson. If a trusted person tells a small child that policemen are pigs who lock people up and kick them, ten years later there will be a young teenager out on the streets who runs away from, rather than towards, the police when a fight starts. If you tell him God is good, the odds are that someday, in trouble, he will pray. If you tell him (or show him) that shoplifting is all right as long as you don't get caught, he will have difficulty forever with the question of personal honesty.

In theory, there should be nothing more satisfying and uplifting than conveying to your child the wisdom that you have spent twenty-five years learning. Some of it is easy. 'Yes, dear, your rabbit died, and his little body will turn into earth and help the flowers to grow', 'Yeast is special stuff that makes the bread rise', or possibly the cop-out, 'When Daddy gets home he'll explain all about how electricity works, I promise. Yes, perhaps he will buy you a potentiometer.' However, as the child gets older and more canny, equally innocent questions begin to turn into ticking time-bombs. More of those later.

And – another pitfall – what about legends? What about Father Christmas, the Tooth Fairy, the gnomes beneath the toadstools? Are you storing up trouble by passing on these tales, which will be proven untrue? Will one falsehood discovered bring down the whole edifice of trust forever? Few of us agonize for very long about such matters, since they become rather rapidly buried under the sordid matters of everyday life, but they are worth considering.

Talking to children is natural and personal. But there are a few universal strategies which make it smoother. To begin with the easiest of the difficult subjects:

Politics It is not too difficult to work out a general attitude to life which is kind, considerate, and socially responsible. We are encouraged to discuss all these things with our children these days: if your four-year-old spots a car bomb in the news, then you find yourself devoting the whole of bathtime to explaining the Irish question to him, outlining the events of the last three hundred years at least.

The trouble is that in a society as politically polarized, as argumentative and chippy as ours, there are several different ways of answering certain questions: you may know what you think, but exactly how much right have you to indoctrinate your child? Or at least, how far must you try to be fair and put the opposite point of view to your own? Try these for size:

'Why are they building a road across the marshes?' 'Well, so that people can get to the new power station faster. You see, the local council is in charge of deciding whether to allow anyone to build a new road or house or factory, and making sure it doesn't spoil anybody else's home. And they decided to build the road. Well, yes, it does spoil our house a bit, and it is a shame about the wild ducks having to go away, but it's very important to have electricity here. Well, Daddy doesn't actually agree, and I know he did say the government is a load of wallies who ought to be pushed off a cliff . . . well, yes, we did sort of choose

them, at least not us, but most people . . . well, not exactly
most people, but – ' (diversion into structure of parliamentary
elections and lack of proportional representation in British politics; child yawns) ' – Well, anyway, they're building a road
because the law says they can. Yes, it's funny that the law says
we can't disturb the wild ducks or shoot them, but the roadmen
are . . . well, that's how it goes . . .'

'Well, no, there isn't a war right now. That air base is there just
in case there might be a war . . . Yes, the Russians have to have
air bases too, because we have, and we've got them because
they have, and . . .'

'Well, Mr Mandela is free now. Yes, they're still fighting,
because . . .'

'Well, you see, some people don't have jobs. They want jobs,
but there aren't any. So they get given some money called
unemployment benefit so they don't actually starve. Yes, it
might be better if they had jobs, but there just aren't any . . .'

The anxiously liberal parent ties himself in knots, bending over
backwards to be fair and let the child see the complexity of
the problem. The angrily committed left-winger abandons the
attempt, takes his child on demonstrations and encourages him
to throw a squeaky rubber Thatcher to the dog. He also, repeat-
edly, says that the government is a bully, a hawk and a philis-
tine, and that it keeps people out of work on purpose. The
staunch right-winger, meanwhile, tells her nicely dressed toddler that the government is quite right to put industrial progress
above wild geese, to negotiate from military strength, and even
– I have had this said to my own children, much to my annoy-
ance – that trade unions are 'mischievous workers who won't
do as they're told' and that people out of work are 'usually
rather lazy'.

But at least all these people – the right, the left, and the
woolly – are trying to explain, and putting a bit of thought into
it. I have stood at the kitchen sink myself trying to explain why

children starve in the Third World while we are throwing out half a stale cake; it wasn't me, I promise, who brought up the subject, it was them, confronted by an Oxfam advertisement. Being able to tell them about Bob Geldof helped a bit; being able to direct them to watching 'Newsround' and 'Blue Peter' also helped. Unashamedly, I give them political explanations which do not always cast a rosy light upon Western civilization; for I think that on the whole, as long as you are a reasonably thoughtful person, there is no point agonizing unduly about whether you are biasing your children unfairly. It is inevitable that they are going to absorb your political attitudes to some extent. We need look no further than a certain corner shopkeeper in Grantham for the origins of Mrs Thatcher's 'goodhousekeeping' and obsession with tidy self-reliance; and to understand Neil Kinnock's political beliefs it helps to cast a thoughtful glance at his mother, the district nurse in a poor area.

But the moments that are really worrying are the ones when – tired or cross or thoughtless – we convey to our children not sincere and well-thought-out beliefs, but appalling, half-conscious prejudices. Everyone has them. The children who taunt black children at school are not doing it out of blind natural instinct: someone has given them a cue that blacks are fair game. That is an extreme: but have you honestly never said in your children's hearing that, say, the Irish are all mad? Or that you can't trust the French? Have you let them go out for walks with a friendly baby-sitter who – excellent though she may be – firmly believes that you will get leukaemia if you buy ice lollies from the Asian corner shop because dusky hands are dirty hands? (A true example, vintage 1986.) Or do your children perhaps boast one of those lovable Grannies who reckons that playing with children from the council estate will invariably give you nits?

Religion It should not be too difficult to communicate your own religion, or lack of it (though it is surprising the number of fashionably agnostic parents who are so afraid of discussing death with their children that they resort, rather shamefacedly,

97

to talking about heaven after all). If your faith is strong and explicit, you need no help from me. However, if you have no more than a vague, generalized, woolly Christianity – the sort of knit-your-own-nativity, white-wedding faith so endemic in Britain – you need to think it over before you start answering questions from small people who trust you.

To reduce it to rock bottom: culturally, it is of considerable importance that children should know the basic Bible stories, the Creation myth, the Nativity and Crucifixion and Resurrection, and the Ten Commandments. If they do not, they lack the basic grammar of Western culture: the vast majority of our plays, novels, poems and paintings will mean very little to them. However, it is up to you whether you teach these things on exact parity with Hinduism, Buddhism and Islam; or even with the legends of Greece and Rome and Ancient Egypt. However determined an agnostic you may be, it would be wise to give the Christian stories a bit of extra consideration: after all, the churches on the landscape and the bishops in the House of Lords are more relevant to your children's life than Isis and

Anubis. In a multiracial area, Diwali and Eid and Chanukkah may be vastly important: but it is curious and rather sad to find – as you do in some British schools – children who have been made able to reel off every detail of these festivals, but allowed to remain hazy about Easter. In the early Seventies, I interviewed some schoolchildren of eight and nine in a highly progressive state primary in Oxfordshire, and discovered that they had no idea who the characters were in the Christmas crib.

It is also important that children pick up the idea of religious tolerance very, very early. My own son was lectured by a six-year-old Jehovah's Witness in his first year at primary school, and informed that the God of school assemblies was actually the Bad Serpent who tempted Eve, and that we were all devil-worshippers. Luckily, he told me instead of letting it fester, and with a deep breath I sprang into a rambling but determined tour of comparative religions: with the emphasis on the idea that different people have seen God differently through the ages, the many names He has been given (from Jehovah to Gitchi Manitou) and the fact (well, I do believe it to be a fact) that if there is one thing God cannot abide it is people fighting over him. With a final coda on the subject of Mister Rushdie having to hide from the Islamic *fatwa*, I let the poor child go back to his Lego bricks.

Legends We have a very useful phrase in our family, dating back to the summer we sailed round Britain recounting every improbable bit of local folklore to the children to pass the time in rain and gales: there were giant codfish washed down chimneys by waves; the Muckle Mester Stoor Worm of Orkney whose liver caught fire and turned into the Iceland volcanoes (his teeth are the Faeroes, Shetlands and Orkneys); the giant buried beneath St Michael's Mount in Cornwall; and so forth. The phrase is this:

> 'It's a legend. A legend is a story that is so old that nobody knows whether it is true or not.'

This, I find, maintains delicious possibilities of giants, enchanters and fairies, without giving them too solid and historical a presence.

However, there are family legends too. Take the Tooth Fairy. We never intended to be bothered with the Tooth Fairy, but when your child comes to you with shining eyes and a bloody little chip of ivory, having learned in the playground what riches may come from the said pixie, it is hard to resist it. So we began: teeth in tinfoil under the pillow, replaced, by morning, with money. Then he began writing notes to the TF, and naturally the TF had to reply (in curly writing). Then, reaching a slightly more sceptical stage (we thought), he and his friends began sprinkling talcum powder on the windowsill to catch the footprints; sure enough, the TF left the little bootprints (pad of finger and pad of thumb: try it). There was a certain advantage to be got from the legend, in that the TF only likes clean teeth, and knows if they've been cleaned after falling out which doesn't count. Tooth after tooth fell, from child after child, and always the money came under the pillow. I rather liked the TF, just as I like Father Christmas: there is something soothing for children in the idea that their own parents are not the sole source of all gifts because the universe is peopled with benevolent beings. It is a primitive sort of religion, and all primitive human beings – like children – need some kind of folk religion.

But when do you stop? I stopped and let the truth be known when I was convinced he knew really. He was seven. I told him it was a legend, but one that didn't work these days, so Dad and I stood in for the TF, just for fun. I really thought he knew already, but disaster: a trembling lip. Didn't want to know. Then he laughed a bit, embarrassedly, and I had a sense of fading magic, dull daylight, premature adulthood. He got over it faster than I did, but I have learned my lesson: after eight Christmases Father Christmas still reigns supreme. He comes down the dining room chimney, and we leave carrots out for the reindeer. And do you know what they do? They eat the carrots and spit the tops down the flue on to the hearth rug, the dirty beasts. FC himself eats a mince pie and leaves strange things: mysterious, wooden, foreign, odd sorts of presents that you don't find in the local newsagent. (You do, however, find them in the Tridias, Tear Fund, and Oxfam catalogues, which is just as well.) I do not know when FC will finally fade, but I have learned the right formula from the astute writer Christina Hardyment, who has raised four daughters:

'Some children at school tell you there is no Father Christmas, do they? What a shame. You see, once children don't believe in Father Christmas any more, he can't come to them. What usually happens is that the parents take over, and fill the stockings instead so nobody is too disappointed. But of course it's never quite as good.'

This is extraordinarily clever. It gives scope for a child to half-believe, or to cling to belief and give it up at his own private pace; and yet not to feel cheated if he spots some wrapping paper that Santa used, or something turns up in his stocking which he saw sticking out of a box under the stairs, or if he actually catches Santa in the act. It keeps the cosmic mystery, and lets it fade without violence into ordinary, parental, loving kindness.

Fears Are intimately connected to all the above subjects. You or anyone else may set them off. Here are some sample fears, from different families:

- That pit bull terriers may hide under the bed and tear your throat out as you sleep (origin: news on television)

- That the Angel of Death will come for the First Born (origin: school bible study)

- That the Tooth Fairy will strangle you (origin obvious: Cure: leave tooth in locked room downstairs.)

- That Father Christmas won't come

- That he *will* come, and be a strange hairy man in the bedroom (origin: fearful department store Santas with bad breath. Cure: stockings hung downstairs.)

- That wishes will come true. This sounds silly, but there was once a fearful moment when a child burst in weeping, 'Do wishes come true?' After some time, it was extracted from him that, 'I just wished that I were a elephant, *but I don't want to be!*'

- That the hole in the ozone layer will drown us or frizzle us all up (talk of scientists working on the problem, the whole world aware of it and working on it, and so on)

- That there will be a New-Kill-ee-ar War (again, speak of goodwill and political work, summit conferences and the universal desire for peace)

- That Mummy and Daddy will die (cure: hugs and reassurance and permission to sleep in your bed till the fear passes)

- That child will die (same cure)

- That sibling will die (same, assisted by pointing out aggressively rude health of sibling. Also worth pointing out in a casual sort of way that just *wishing* someone was dead never ever works. Fear probably has its origin in just such a wish.)

- That burglars will get in (show off locks, bolts, and such with great gravitas)

- That witches, goblins, ghosts and devils will get in through the walls (a tricky one. Merely saying they don't exist may not work. Once I had a visiting child who terrified mine with tales of witches that came in to Get You. Unable to calm any of them down, and getting desperate for some sleep myself, I reverted to my Catholic childhood and showed them a crucifix which happened to be on the wall, and a picture of

St Brendan in his boat, explaining that no evil thing could come where a holy picture was. It worked instantly. The only problem was that the visiting child went home and told his mummy – and the whole neighbourhood – that at my house we went to sleep holding a crucifix to keep vampires off.

I could go on forever. Any mother could. A few children have no such fears, or at least not many; some have a new one every night. The important thing is to keep the lines of communication open: always listen to fears, however daft and repetitive. If they are sad universal fears (like being homeless, or unloved, or orphaned, or caught in a war) it is curiously helpful to tell the child that everyone gets these feelings sometimes, even grown-ups, and that you get used to chasing them away. This creates a comradeship, and a healthy sense that it is not the disaster which is the real enemy, but the *feeling* of impending disaster.

If they are wildly improbable fears, you shouldn't laugh, or go all psychological and automatically relate them to the birth of a sibling, a house-move, or any of the other reliable old chestnuts. These may have a bearing too, but the fears themselves are worth respecting. Try to trace them back to their source. One small boy was depressed for days about his father's impending six-week business trip. It turned out that he had misheard it as a six-*year* trip, poor little devil. My own daughter developed a fear of sleeping in her own bedroom, and we alternately raged and coaxed her in vain. After she had taken to sleeping in various rooms in rotation, dragging her white teddy and duvet with her on a restless royal progress like a small Queen Elizabeth, I went one night into her own bedroom. Downstairs, my husband was watching television, and a trailer came on for some tawdry thriller. 'I'll kill you – I swear it' hissed a voice, curiously amplified through the floor. My poor little child had been suffering night after night, from a sinister approximation to the techniques of sleep-learning. The tacky, violent, sensational television culture had been invading her rest. No wonder she went walkabout.

15. Below the Belt: And bum to you, too

Warning: this chapter contains explicit words which may well prove shocking and disturbing to readers over eight years old. Be prepared. Brace yourself. It deals with bottoms. And potties. It may include willies, poo-poos, and the breaking of wind. It will be, I promise you, a positive relief when it gets back in to the safe adult areas of sex and reproduction: before that comes a great murky area of deliberate offence. Not deliberate on my part, of course; but on the children's, certainly. For there is a phenomenon to examine.

Years ago, in the heyday of the singing duo Flanders and Swann, they had a smash hit song which began, in falsetto childish tones:

'Mother's out, father's out, let's talk rude!'

and had a chorus of

'Pee, poo, belly, bum, drawers!'

And they got it entirely right. Nothing is so beguiling to little children as potty talk, botty talk, smut, filth – call it what you will. It has always been fascinating, and I fear it always will be. Certainly there was never much hope for those enlightened, earnest parents in the 1960s who thought that a modern atmosphere of openness and frankness about bodily functions would make smutty giggling a thing of the past. The most uninhibited family I ever knew went in for this sort of openness: Mummy and Daddy walking around naked, free discussion of bowels and the birth process. Yet one day I called to find dear little Nellie, aged five, dancing around the kitchen chanting:

> 'Piddle in the pot, nice and steaming hot,
> coming out yer bot!'

while her mother gritted her teeth in a desperate attempt not to look shocked. 'I don't know why she does it,' she said plaintively. 'We've always treated urination as quite natural, and I haven't the faintest idea who taught her to call it' – she spat the word out – '*piddle*. Really, it's so silly and vulgar.'

I commiserated politely, while Nellie continued her little song. But deep down I already suspected that her mother was struggling in vain. Now, with children of my own, I know it. The truth is that in every small child there is a streak of something profoundly and inevitably silly and vulgar. Among adults, after all, we refer to smutty jokes as 'childish' or 'infantile', and if children cannot be infantile, who can? I am not at all sure that we ought to try and stop them. The rudery will out, somehow: if we do manage to prevent them from voicing it in their own home, we are not instilling tasteful and modest standards in them. We are just teaching them to bottle it up. Ban all poo-talk at home, and they will assemble in the school playground to chant 'Farty party, farty party'. Or go round to their friends' houses for a hilarious recitation of of 'Mummy, Mummy, I'm not happy, something heavy in my nappy.'

I know this, because we as parents have taken a benevolently lax attitude to potty jokes, and our house has therefore become the Poo-Talk capital of East Suffolk. More restrainedly brought-up children flock here for tea, take my children into a corner and murmur, 'Smelly Knickers at the Vicar's!' with gales of indecorous laughter. If you ignore it, they eventually stop, but it can seem a long, long time.

Some of it, however, is quite interesting. When a child returns from school and declaims:

> 'Fatty and Skinny went to the zoo
> Fatty fell into some elephant's poo
> Skinny ran home to tell his mum
> But all he got was a kick up the bum!'

It is not particularly edifying – not the image of family life and respect for the animal world which one would have chosen to impart – but nonetheless it rhymes and scans, and has a certain reckless combination of grotesquery, muck and anarchy which puts it firmly in the tradition of Rabelais. It is a sort of satire, quite a respectable literary form really. Or so I tell myself, trying not to giggle into the kitchen-towel holder. In strolls my son to observe that

> 'My friend Billy had a ten-foot willy
> He showed it to the lady next door
> She thought it was a snake and hit it with a rake
> And now it's only six foot four.'

Why they do this is no particular mystery. Psychologists warn us, direly, that children are frightened and awed by the power of their natural functions. Ever since Freud, a lot of emotional significance has been attached to potty-training, constipation and so on. It could be that the jokes are just the children's way of defusing their own Freudian love-hate relationship with the lavatory. Think that if it makes you feel better about it. Or it could be that perhaps – perish the thought – all these things actually *are* quite funny. As is sex. After all, they remind us at the height of our human pretensions and pomposities that we have an inescapable animal nature. Who can blame the children for giggling at the idea that the Queen might break wind?

Therefore one plays it cool. However, there are limits. Few spectacles are more hilarious than a liberated, open family which keeps telling its children that there is nothing wrong with the body and nudity, suddenly faced with explaining precisely why one does not, in polite society, take out one's willy and wave it at Great-Auntie Flo. The best approach (as for the best anti-molester message) is:

'Bottoms are Private.'

Speech, however, is free. And another limit worth considering is on the words you teach children. When they are seven or eight, and developing a decent sense of modesty, they may as well learn the right ones: penis, vagina, anus, and so on. But, before then, consider: is it not better to use childish words for purely social reasons? Here I diverge from advanced childcare gurus, but considering that small children are going to use scatological words as insults anyway, would you not rather be called a 'Poo-Face!' than a 'S***head?' And will Granny not respond more forgivingly to a cry of 'I hate your smelly bum!' than to one of 'I hate your rotten old vagina!' (That is a real example. The child didn't mean anything, just knew the word was something bottomy. But it took the daughter-in-law two years to live it down.) Think about it. Another useful motto is:

'Bottom jokes are only all right in the family!'

although this may lead to some hair-splitting about grannies, aunts of varying susceptibilities, and whether it is all right to say 'wee-wee' to an uncle by marriage.

And so to sex. The old way of tackling the subject is to leave it strictly alone until puberty, and then harrumph a bit about birds and bees and Impure Thoughts. This no longer works, for the simple reason that if you won't answer a straight question their schoolteacher will, or the television will convey a confusing idea that babies come from kissing people with your head sideways, or some schoolfriend will give your baffled chick such a tangled picture of reproduction that she vows (as I did, aged eight) to observe perpetual celibacy.

Par contraire, the post-1960s way of teaching sex is to bombard the child from an early age with technicalities, medical words, and cheery little books that say an orgasm is 'like a great big sneeze' (speak for yourself). Here, the drawback is that the child will get bored and stop listening, or else cause violent embarrassment by discussing big sexy sneezes with inappropriate adults.

The third way is simply to answer questions in a pleasant, straightforward, unembarrassed manner as and when they occur to the child. Unfortunately, they generally seem to occur in the middle of a supermarket checkout queue, in a chemist's shop full of cross old ladies, in the doctor's waiting-room, or on a bus. You could always fob the child off with 'I'll explain when we get home', but it depends on the child. The only safeguard against unconvincing floundering is to run through it on your own before the subject ever comes up. Ready?

'Women have a little house in their tummy that the baby grows up in. It's called the womb. And they've got special places called ovaries, and once a month a teeny weeny egg . . .'

'Men grow special seeds in their bodies, and the seed can come out of their willy and meet the egg in the mummy . . .'

'When a baby's big enough to be born and live safely, it has to get out of the mummy. It comes out of a special hole . . .'

Difficult, isn't it? I would not dream of putting words into anyone's mouth, but a private run-through in your own mind will save a lot of confusion and floundering when you get asked. The trick is not to answer anything which hasn't been asked: leave the Fallopian tubes, testicles, ovaries and perversions for a bit later, and stick to such topics as babies growing up in mummies' wombs, seeds coming from daddies, and the fact that mummies and daddies love each other and want to build a baby out of that love (astonishingly accepted by all children I know, even when Daddy is nowhere in sight).

As to discussing the act of sex itself, I may be stoned to death by sexologists for saying so, but after a cursory and boring explanation of the mechanics ('The seed gets into the mummy by a special kind of hug that only grown-ups can do'), I have always loftily tried to convey a general sense that sex is something grown-up mummies and daddies do which is not particularly relevant or interesting to children. After all, there are many odd things adults do which their offspring wouldn't fancy: drinking bitter coffee, talking to yakky ladies in shops, writing out cheques, listening to the weather forecast. One more peculiar taste is neither here nor there.

One other thing. If you are anxious yourself, or unsatisfied, or under sexual siege in some way; if you are equivocal about sex, or angry at the mess it has made of your life, or merely fascinated by it all day long, then that is your burden. It is not your child's. To lay it on him, or to let him grow up in a hothouse atmosphere laden with sexual innuendo is a form of abuse. And it may lead to other forms: all children are at some risk of sexual abuse, but 'knowing' children are at graver risk than most. Treat with caution anyone – even a therapist – who goes on too much about the 'awakening sexuality' of young children. Far safer to stick to the boring old lines: you belong to yourself, you don't have to hug anyone you don't feel like' hugging, or in a way you don't feel like doing it, and bottoms are private.

Though it does no harm to admit that they have their funny side too.

16. Party Politics: Taking the cake

Children's parties are the stuff of dreams and nightmares. The dream sequence shows a dozen little faces around a long table, a cake shaped like a train with Swiss-roll wheels, the soft light of candles and the piping of childish voices singing 'Happy Birthday' before filing out to Pass the Parcel with little squeaks of happy (yet somehow well-controlled) excitement.

The nightmare is of an invading rabble of screaming, cake-throwing delinquents. It is that you will be left single-handed with a fighting scrum of uncivilized infants, with the local asthmatic being crushed at the centre and your own birthday girl wailing dismally on the fringes.

Now, I like parties, and incline to optimism. I also have a house which suits children's parties (old, battered, devoid of fitted carpets and not too recently painted). So far it has seen twelve birthday parties, six Christmas teas, two impromptu children's garden-parties in summer and a special mini-party held at ten minutes' notice for those younger siblings not invited to someone else's sixth birthday party. When the inevitable day comes when my children start to groan in a sophisticated, sub-teenage manner and ask for theatre outings and burger sessions in some plastic clip-joint instead of a proper party, I shall be mortally offended, and probably insist they have a real one at home too. With jelly.

I rationalize this with a lot of high-flown stuff about how children need to get some idea of formal social occasions as young as possible, in case one day they get asked to Buckingham Palace. But the truth is that, given a Thomas the Tank Engine tablecloth and a boxful of party squeakers, there is no stopping me. I become uncontrollably keen and throw myself into the proceedings with indecent zest.

However, I too have scars. There are ground rules to observe, and I have broken them all in the past. Remember that simply putting a lot of children in a room with some balloons does not constitute an instant party. It will create instant tears. You need organization: a mother is an impresario, and a good party is a performance. It is a three-act drama, involving a lot of improvisation around a basic script. Here is that basic script.

Act I: The Games Invitations should always give a start time and a stop time – 3.30 to 5.30 p.m., for instance. Ideally, all the guests should arrive bang on time, and a game should begin as soon as their coats are off. This especially applies to four- and five-year-olds' parties: older children have more capacity for standing around chatting and opening presents without either losing their nerve or starting a fight. Mothers who dawdle along late are a nuisance. And if mothers have to stay (some younger children insist) they should refrain from chattering, interfering, or generally spoiling the ambience. You do, however, need to bag one of them as an assistant for taking children to the lavatory, retying hair bows on the fussier girls, and clapping plasters on wounds.

111

The first game ought to involve jumping up and down. This relieves tension, and ensures that anyone who wants to go to the loo develops the symptoms nice and early, before tea. Musical bumps, statues, or chairs fit the bill nicely. Next, for children over four I rather favour a more structured game, something that fits the theme of the party – pirates or circuses or ballerinas or whatever. (By the way, if you have a fancy dress theme party, make sure you have a few spare pirate kerchiefs, clown hats or whatever – there is always one child whose mother hasn't read the invitation or who has a new baby and keeps forgetting everything.)

These games are easier once the children have had a term at school: it is quite wonderful how, from being a big amorphous threatening mass, a group of sixteen children is miraculously turned into a Class. Once they have been at school you can have complicated games that need explaining: merely clap your hands decisively and say 'NOW! Everyone is a pirate. There are two teams of pirates. Make two teams – red and blue, here are your rosettes – now the job is to find the treasure . . .' and so on. Before school age, keep it simple. We had a howling success with a tracking exercise involving party streamers snaking around the house, leading them up climbing frames and down slides, through a makeshift tunnel, in one door and out the other, to a pirate island full of chocolate coins.

More recently, I went through a non-competitive phase and devised a game with no winners at all. The idea was that they were astronauts on a space mission to help a lot of wounded space monsters. Each child had a piece of card representing part of an octopus's tentacle: each set of clues and stick-on green footprints led to a mutilated cardboard octopus in a different room, and they had to complete it by tessellating their pieces on until it was complete. Without every single child's piece the stages couldn't be completed, so the big ones kept a sharp eye on the small, confused ones who kept threatening to lose their bits of card.

The game was a success. I like to think it was because it brought out qualities of non-competitiveness and cooperation; but reluctantly admit that the success could have something to do with the less idealistic aspect, which was that in one of the rooms they were pounced on by my husband, dressed as a six-foot-tall, green, furry, squawking parrot. It always pays to have a few surprises up your sleeve.

Act II: The Tea Anyone can lay on a children's party tea. I would not insult your intelligence by suggesting menus, except to point out that there are certain children who hate all sweet things and need sausages, crisps and cheese straws. Also that some children like sandwiches with no butter. Otherwise, do as you please: either spend eight hours making witches' hats out of ice cream and cakes with little faces on, or else nip down to the supermarket and buy the lot.

More serious is the problem of some children who have never had the experience of sitting down to a meal in company, because they are normally fed in front of the television or on the hoof. Such children may respond wonderfully to a pretty table with candles and crackers on it; or they may ruin everyone else's dignified formal tea by getting down and running around. A touch of firmness is needed. I can confirm that a six-foot-tall, green, fur parrot is an invaluable disciplinary force: one squawk and down they sit.

The Cake is of course vital. Although, frankly, small children get so het up at parties that they rarely eat it, so you might as well ice a shoebox. Ask any child what it wants its cake to represent and the answer will probably be 'a combine harvester' or 'a ballerina on her points', and unless you are Jane Asher you are banjaxed. The trick is to steer the conversation round to something you can do, like a circus ring (round and flat) or a Swiss-roll train. My best effort so far has been a galleon: not as hard as it sounds. I got a friend to make two lumps of her patent ultra-dense sculptable sponge cake, shaped the bow and stern, lashed on the butter icing and Polo mint portholes, and rigged the whole thing with pencils and string (let nobody tell you that everything on a cake needs to be edible. If you are a genius with moulding-icing, then bully for you. Idle and feckless women like myself can get away with pencils, elastic bands, and bowsprits made of raw spaghetti. You're going to be super-

113

vising the eating of this cake more closely than any other of the year, so there is ample chance to whip off the inedible bits.) The great moment was when we lit the candles and the rigging caught fire.

Act III: The Riot Tea is a jolly event, and it breaks the ice. However, ice can be useful stuff. It holds raging waters in check, and raging children too. If you rashly leave a game like Pass the Parcel until after tea, you may end up with your orderly circle turning into a heaving, struggling, shrieking mass of mixed infants and ripped newspaper. Pass the Parcel is a dodgy business anyway: they get bored, even if you put a sweet in between each layer. We jazzed it up by making it Pass the Octopus at the space party (pull of a tentacle every time, sweet in tentacle) but even so it palled. Some jazz it up even further with silly forfeits like 'do a somersault', or 'sing a song'. But whether or not you play more games after tea, the Riot is inevitable.

There are two ways of handling it. You can hand the riot over to a professional children's entertainer, with a Punch and Judy show or a collection of magic tricks. There is something ineffably soothing in hearing a voice in the next room saying, with that steely authority they have, 'Are you all happy children?', and hearing an obedient chorus of 'Yeeeess!' However, under-fives may collapse in hysterical terror if the entertainer is even remotely frightening, and if he isn't, he may be unable to contain the seething, bubbling Riot that is waiting to happen. The only way to find a good entertainer is by personal recommendation, or by taking the risk of having your party end in chaos or anticlimax. If I could find a cheerful chap who would come with a guitar and lead a decent ordinary sing-song, I would opt for that instead.

The other solution to the after-tea problem is to channel the riot into a new direction of your own. One year Paul was dressed up as a bear and we inaugurated the game of chase-the-bear-and-tie-him-up in party streamers. It went very well, with shrieks of terror and delight in equal proportions. At another family's party, a wolf galloped about and the children were issued with water pistols to hunt him (it was in the garden). Once Paul was dressed up as a clown and the children were allowed to splat crazy-foam custard pies into his face. These events were chaotic and cathartic, as all good parties should be. But on the whole, I would not recommend starting them earlier than twenty minutes before official chucking-out time. When the mothers turn up and find their little darlings covered in streamers and foam and butter-icing, they can take them away for a nice quiet bath.

Epilogue: The Party Bag This is a fine art. The trick is to put things into the bag which will give pleasure to the children, surprise them and keep them happy for a while, without spending too much money (even if you have it. Raise the expectations too much, and the other mothers will be justifiably cross with you). I work on the basis of one small packet of sweets or chocolate figure, one balloon, a squeaker if one is left over, one incredibly cheap object (like a tiny pencil, or revolting 5p plastic bracelet) and one cheapish but very interesting thing. I collect these (see TOYS p. 78) all year round. The attic is always full of peculiar fibre-optic miniature torches, hopping false teeth, rainbow spectacles and impenetrable magic boxes.

Finally, **The Guest Star** Somewhere among your friends' children, there must exist a child (often a boy) who is never frightened, never fazed, totally gregarious and ready for anything. Whether your child likes him or not, *get him booked*. I would never have a party without a certain Patrick, because I know that if I say brightly, 'Now then, let's have a race pushing ping pong balls with your noses', Patrick will be down there, bum in the air, before I can finish the sentence. And the others will follow. If I say, 'Who can jump highest?', Patrick will be through the ceiling. If a smaller child doesn't know how to play musical bumps, she has only to watch Patrick falling like a stone to the floor, and she will get the hang of it immediately. Here's to Patrick, and all the Patricks everywhere. In years to come they will be the toast of some West End nightspot and the darlings of the gossip columns: and who can grudge them their fame?

17. And so to School: What, neurotic? Me?

Every now and again, you read about one of those families where the parents have decided against sending the children to school. They use their legal freedom to educate them at home and sometimes with spectacular success. At the best, the home educators are inspired, dedicated and wise. At the worst, they are raving cranks. Some turn to kitchen-table lessons for the very good reason that they tried school, and it didn't suit their child; but a good number, the ones that fascinate me most, keep their children out of school on principle, from the start.

In the year before my first child started school, I read everything I could about home education. Like many parents of bright, keen, happy, original and sensitive four-year-olds (well, aren't they all?), I dreaded the idea of handing him over to an institution. I thought it a shame to put him into a group four times bigger than anything he knew, and toss him into the playground jungle where terrifying-looking children kicked footballs and jumped on one another shouting 'Gertcha!' I now know that this is silly, and that every one of those children is someone's sensitive little baby, and that most of the rough-housing takes place between enthusiastically consenting bigger boys; but the experience of trundling one's little precious baby in its pushchair past the average primary playground is distinctly harrowing.

More seriously, I remembered the endless time-wasting of school life: why should my boy waste his brightest learning years in a queue of twenty, handing in dinner money, answering registers, waiting for permissions?

Many of us have our own jungly memories of school: frightening whisperers in the corner who plot against you, cruel names called, sly pinches in Assembly, the burning unfairness of teachers who tell off the wrong culprit because they didn't

116

quite see what happened. We are cowed by ancient instincts: we go down to the school as confident, assertive, well-adjusted adults to grill the head teacher, and one whiff of the old school-dinnery, chalky, plasticeny atmosphere reduces us to nervous children again. We project such fears on to our sons and daughters: little Freddie may have spent all his life so far in family houses, or cosy Playgroup Portakabins: what is he going to make of this great barn of a building, its ugliness, its echoes? We tremble in sympathy, even as we brightly try to talk our child through the first visits with syrupy praise of his Lovely Teacher and the Lovely Paints and Toys. Oh woe, oh woe, how will my baby cope?

Cheer up. Baby will probably cope better than you: if, that is, you are going through any of the above anxieties. You may not be. I deliberately began this chapter negatively, because I began my own school-mother career negatively, and have since been converted. Forgive me if you are an optimistic parent of a confident child who feels, or has felt, no misgivings: those of us who do suffer them have a need to acknowledge it. Besides, why not begin from a standpoint of doubt? Anything is good if it sharpens your sense of responsibility in choice, of watchful-

ness over the school, and constructive empathy with the bewildered child now starting. It is bad to communicate your disquiet to the child, of course, but that is only one more reason to work through the fears systematically and eliminate them before the actual first days. If you put on a bright act and pretend to yourself and your spouse that you are 'looking forward to getting the days back', while secretly you are weeping for a finished babyhood, the odds are that the only person who picks up the vibrations will be the child.

So, deal with your reservations. Choose well, start well, manage the change well. Stay confident. Primary education in schools does, on the whole, work wonders.

Choosing a school Even if your local state primary has the best reputation in the country, go to see it (without the child), and then visit another possible school, state or private. It is the best way to get a 'feel' for schools. Otherwise there is a risk of either being dazzled by the niceness of the place (not realizing that all primary school classrooms are rather nice places to be – children do furnish a room); or being horrified by aspects of it which are, again, shared by all schools (like the racket). You should be able to approve of the school on several grounds:

- *Educational* It is rare to find a very bad primary school in Britain except in overcrowded, understaffed schools in underprivileged areas. There are, however, a great many which are only middling. If the national curriculum is in force, ask how many children are reaching the 'attainment targets'; try and look at the workbooks for evidence of interested teachers and close attention; ask casual questions like 'at what age do you think they should be reading fluently alone?', and judge the answers. Look at the work up on the walls: does it inspire, is it well-presented and lovingly pasted up by children and teachers who are proud of it? Then drop in again ten days later and see if the display has changed. If not, smell a rat.

  Be wary of private schools which make great boasts about homework schedules and starting all the pupils on Latin and

118

French at five, and of state schools which talk of *nothing* but attainment-targets and reading-ages. On the other hand, be equally wary of schools which tell you that 'formal' subjects don't matter at all and that tests are meaningless. The golden truths of education lie somewhere between these extremes. The fact is that there are two possible, but opposing, disasters: if you push children too hard at an early age it will apparently work – they can parrot things and write neatly – but may turn out disastrously for them later, when they burn out and become sullen non-achieving secondary pupils. Yet it is equally disastrous, depressing for them and gloomy for the future, if the school is so soft or so short-staffed that an averagely intelligent child reaches the age of nine hardly even reading. Try to talk about the golden mean with the head teacher. If you dislike the answers, think carefully.

- *Atmosphere and tone* are equally important. Is it a nice school? Does it make you feel confident and friendly and interested? Are people smiling? Do the children seem relaxed? This is the moment to discard all educational considerations and trust your instinct all the way. Some schools feel dull and sour and restrictive; some feel wild and disorganized and rough. The good ones have a sort of hum about them, impossible to define but obvious when it is absent. I never step through our local school's ugly glass doors without feeling immediately better and more relaxed, livelier and benevolent towards the world. This tone is set by the teachers, and carried through by the non-teaching staff, secretary, dinner ladies and above all the children themselves. When you visit, try not to waste time pouring out all your own theories and hopes in a torrent of chat: listen to the teachers, hope that they get interrupted by other staff and children while you are talking to them, see how they speak to one another: is there respect, affection, mutual help and interest? Try to talk to friends' children at the school already, but casually, to see how they view it. At this age they should not yet be into the older habit of jeering at teachers and joking about them in a *Beano* fashion, but should refer to

119

them as respected friends most of the time. You may also want to consider religion, and (if that way inclined) social 'tone'; but neither of these things will help unless the school has that basic, magic, ineffable Hum.

- *Convenience* It matters more than you think. You may find two schools which are both almost ideal, except that one will involve your child in an extra hour a day – or more – travelling in a car or bus, stuck in a London traffic jam or snaking down icy rural roads. The farther school may involve a shared school run, and the possibility that you yourself will rarely be the smiling face at the school gate. Unless the nearer school is really unacceptable, think seriously before you commit yourself and your child to the distant option. Think of bringing friends home for tea, of parties and outings; think of winter mornings, think of the waste of time on hot summer afternoons in a car. Only then can you judge whether the slight edge the other school offers is worth it.

Starting Good schools usually offer four-year-olds the chance to spend a few afternoons in class during the term before they enter. Let me tell you, however, that even if a child hugely enjoys these and seems utterly settled, the first real schoolday might turn out somewhat differently. At our school, a blanket of care wrapped itself around my son from the first: the other children were kind and welcoming, the teachers warm, the routines unthreatening and he loved his pre-school visits. Nonetheless, when September came he cried bitterly every day for two weeks: daily his little fingers had to be prised off my sleeve, and daily I went away (almost weeping myself) to catch wrong trains or put laundry away in the oven. It was hard, very hard, not to give in to his impassioned pleas to leave. I was determined to keep on at it, and even invoked the Law, explaining that he didn't have a choice and nor did I: the only thing which cheered him up was a promise that we would let him leave at sixteen instead of eighteen.

Well, not *quite* the only thing. What was apparent, and what helped us to keep up the torture for that terrible fortnight, was the clear fact that his mind was being exercised in a way it had not been before. Each night in the bath, as he wailed, 'I don't wanter go to schoo-ool tomorrow,' he would keep stopping and saying things like, 'But if the moon is all sandy and dry, how does it shine?' or 'Mummy, do you know that water has weight?' School and its ways of learning were broadening him, new people were getting a chance to plant nuggets of information and ideas and different views of the world in his mind. I felt that school would work, was working already, and that he would soon realize it.

Which he did. I am not sure how long I would have kept up the steady compulsion, the agonized handover at the school gate, but gradually the teachers began to report the crying becoming briefer and briefer once he got inside. One morning I said, 'Don't cry, it upsets the other children.' (Oddly enough, it didn't. They seemed to accept it as a mannerism, and still kept coming up to show him their toys even at the height of his hysteria.) He looked up casually and said an astonishing thing: 'Oh. Do they think it's serious crying, then?' I could have shaken him. The crying had somehow mutated into being – well, nothing but a mannerism after all. He stopped, and has loved school since.

This, of course, may not happen to you and it didn't happen to us with the second child. But if it does, be resolute: give it time. Discuss it with the teachers, trust them, stay calm. A lot of the panic may stem not from real dislike of school, but from dislike of change. This is, after all, a great rite of passage and some people greet such rites – even weddings – with tears.

Ways to ease the start, for any child, are:

- Check up on the nuts-and-bolts of his new day. Try to get an idea of its shape: explain about assembly, and playtime, and school dinner, but only in general terms. Tell him that there is no harm in asking, however many times you have to repeat the same question; tell him that nobody will mind.

- Discuss in advance such things as how you ask for a lavatory (usually 'toilet' in schools). Make sure he is good at going

121

alone: organize a practice on some strange public lavatories to increase his sang-froid.

- Make sure he can cope with his clothes. Some schools have the tiresome and silly habit of putting five-year-olds in uniform ties and shoelaces and shirts with cuff buttons. Serve them right if it takes half an hour to dress a class for PE. The ideal costume for school, quite frankly, is a tracksuit with a floppy neck and without tight ankle cuffs. Shoes that close with Velcro are a godsend.

- Talk of your own schooldays with enthusiasm, remembering only the most harmless sorts of fun. Nicholas's early days were made more bearable by a very dull but reassuring story of how his father spent the whole of his first day of school sitting in a wooden rocking swan. We did not tell him about my early days. Well, yes, you guessed it: I screamed too.

- If you can find him a friend who is starting at the same time, that is good. An older friend already there is even better: my thanks, now and formally, to Matthew for all he did in those first weeks. Siblings are best of all: so thanks to Nicholas also, for what he did, in turn, for his sister Rose two years later.

- Learn the ropes yourself. Find out where to wait outside at home-time, and how to send in dinner-money or PE kit. DO NOT BE LATE arriving, or the child will feel awkward and guilty; and DO NOT BE LATE at home-time either. Remember that you are, for the moment, the only fixed star in a shifting universe.

- Don't grill the poor child every day about what happened and what he did. He might just want peace and quiet and to forget it all. But if he tells you, listen.

Managing Like so much else in parenthood, being a school-child's mother is a management skill. There are things to learn:

- Not only do you have to get into the habit of remembering dinner-money on Mondays, PE kit on Tuesdays, library books on Fridays, to put the reading book back in the red folder with its marker in, and so on; but you have to get into the habit of searching your child every day, satchel and pockets, for notes sent back by the ubiquitous school system of 'Pupil Post'. These may be absolutely vital information about end of term, parents' nights, plays, or other things you must not miss. They may be appeals for costumes, or junk for the science room, or tedious exhortations about searching your child for nits: whatever they are, you need to read them. However, some children go on forgetting to hand them over until they are seven or eight years old. Search.

- Try to adapt to the new day. Working mothers, however part-time, will find to their dismay that it is actually harder to organize life around a schoolchild than it was around a toddler. If you are away, for example, on a long day-trip or even longer, leaving a toddler with a nanny or minder, you can get back full of enthusiasm and promise a full programme of fun and togetherness at the swimming pool or wherever the next day. A schoolchild just has to get up and go to school. With a young child, you can be flexible about shopping trips or lunch with friends, saying 'yes' to impulsive suggestions. Having a schoolchild means that you are tied down hard to that very difficult mid-afternoon time when the school doors open; and that you will be in heavy demand for the subsequent hour or so as the child unwinds. I know women who have actually given up jobs when primary school started, because of these pressures. 'Her hours at home seem so few now that I need to be there,' said one. She took a part-time job instead, in the mornings.

- The first two terms are not the time to take on a new job yourself unless you have to. Remember that there will be illnesses: no school. There will be half-terms and holidays: no school. There will be strange random days on which the teachers have to be retrained for some new Government curriculum initiative: suddenly, no school. Develop a network of friends among other mothers for emergencies.

- Parents' evenings or the equivalent also demand new skills. There is a fine line to tread between being pushy and aggressive, 'Why is Sarah Jane only on Book 3? She should be on Book 5 at least, surely?', and being too obsequious with teachers. You know your child best, but they know the mechanisms of learning best. It is vital that you work together. Ask the teacher if there is anything you can do to help, at home, such as following a particular system of reading together, or playing games that would help with maths. If you don't understand a particular teaching system (new maths is baffling, team-teaching very baffling, and even Look and Say reading can seem alien to older parents), then ask to have it explained to you. If there isn't time ask if you can borrow a textbook for teachers, or at least get the name of some educational text which would make it clear what they are trying to do. Don't stay in the dark if you are bothered about a subject: but don't shout down methods just because you haven't heard of them. Try to find out what other friends' children are doing at different schools, but not in an aggressive or competitive way.

- Getting involved in the school yourself can be wonderfully rewarding, and is quite the best way of learning something real about it, and regaining a sense of proportion by meeting other children than your own, at different ages. Many schools like parent-helpers to join in the classroom – hearing little ones read, or doing craftwork in workshops. If you want to offer your time, do it on a regular basis if possible, in a decent spirit of humility and helpfulness. Never forget that you are an amateur. Mind you, from my experience of doing it once a week this past year, an hour with a group of someone else's seven-year-olds will ensure that you never, for a moment, forget your amateur status.

  During the first year, try not to be directly involved with

your own child at school if you can help it. It confuses them. After that they think it is quite fun, and call you 'Miss' like the other children do.

- Take the business of reading seriously, but not too seriously. You can help by having books around, reading aloud with pleasure in the evenings, and heaping praise on a child who tries to spell out the cereal packet to you; but you can't help by pushing. All children learn to read at different speeds, and the pernicious doctrine of 'reading ages' only serves to panic parents of slower developers. There is no proof whatever that the child who reads fluently at three and a half is any better, or keener, at seven than the one who has only been at it a year. *Do not* get yourself, or your child, into a quite unnecessary state just because the little toad next door is alleged to be reading alone. If the school tells you there is no real problem, believe them. If you don't trust them, then get a respectable educational psychologist – if you must – to have a chat with your child informally. Try not to tie your child into any tests or exams for new schools during the period when he is learning to read at his own pace: tests are very unforgiving, and rarely allow for differences between individuals.

  Above all – and it is desperately hard when you are worried – *do not nag*. Reading is a private pleasure, sometimes a subversive one. It should be something you do to get *away* from your parents nagging you. The real breakthrough will have come, not when your child drones out a page of faultless school text to you, but when he slips away to his room to be peacefully alone with a book. The pushiest, most academically neurotic parents I know have got a child who reads beautifully, but never for pleasure: he is hooked on videos. Don't do it.

Siblings The division between pre-schooler and schoolchild is the most definite change in life since birth: it cannot be compared to any other huge step – walking, talking, even playgroup – because it is so all-encompassing and final. From the first moment at school, a child is committed day after day, week after week, for years, to a waking life mainly dominated by school and the friends made there. She is under new disciplines: lining up, waiting her turn, hanging up her coat on the right peg, carrying a project through without losing concentration. After the utter freedom of being a toddler pottering about in the kitchen or backyard, school is quite a shock – even when it is a pleasant one. The old friends and siblings left behind have no idea of what is going on in the schoolchild's life: it can create strains in their small social world.

Handle it carefully. Close-born children (two years' gap or less) are difficult to reconcile at this stage. At 3.30 p.m. daily you have an elder child who is exhausted and wants your undivided attention, and a younger one who is jealous and can't see what all the fuss is about. Real antagonisms can develop. To help resolve them, encourage the big one to 'play school' with the little one, thus assuaging her curiosity and providing useful scope for bossing (the big one needs to boss. She feels very small and insignificant at the moment).

There may be nasty moments when the eldest brings home a schoolfriend and behaves in a foully macho and exclusive manner, setting traps for the little one and making war – again, to get rid of that dreadful sense of lowliness. Grit your teeth: it settles down in the end.

Younger friends-next-door are also a problem. If Rosamund and Chloe have played together four times a week ever since they were babies, but Rosamund is nine months older, there may be a whole year when she is at school and Chloe isn't. Chloe is going to be bored and restless all day if she hasn't enough other friends. And, more distressing still, she will be over-keen to come round at 3.30 p.m. However, poor old Rosamund is less keen. A child who has been solitary all day is overtaxing company for one who has been struggling bravely in a crowd since 8.45 a.m. Chloe wants fun, games, running about and confidences. Rosamund just wants to sit on Mummy's knee and be very quiet. Result, misery all round.

Time is the only cure. After the first weeks, Rosamund will relax and may quite enjoy the undemanding company of her little friend after school. But you have to be prepared for the old toddler alliances to break off completely. From now on, your child will be making all sorts of decisions and friendships without your help. But never close the doors entirely: some baby friendships revive against all odds.

Troubles There will be times of trouble, at school. There may be another child who oppresses yours, even unconsciously ('I apsley *hate* Joanna'). There may be real bullying. More likely, there may be difficulties in making friends (see chapter on 'First Friends'), and loneliness in a playground full of gangs and alliances. There may be misunderstandings with teachers, smarts of injustice, or largely unfounded dreads and fears of a particular teacher. We had hysteria every Thursday morning for months about one teacher Nicholas was afraid of: I have seldom met a milder, more tolerant woman. We believe it was her hairstyle, which reminded him of someone he didn't like.

All these problems need talking about: with the child, in a tone of interest and concern (but not overemphatic sympathy, not 'It's a shame! Aaah! How dare she!'). Also with the teachers at school. If you have chosen well, and your school has a good happy atmosphere and a real concern for the whole child, they will want to help you sort it out. Try to do it calmly: if you have been up half the night with a weeping child, it will take very ounce of self-control, humour and detachment you can muster, but you *must* listen to the teacher's viewpoint as well as putting forward your own. A story which came to you about a bigger child knocking yours over and trampling on his hat may have reached the staff quite differently: possibly as an account of your child kicking the other one on the shins and tearing up his birthday card. Your child's allegation that a teacher told her off for something she didn't do needs even more tact and diplomacy to sort out. But it can be done: if it can't, perhaps the school was the wrong one after all. Remember, if your child is unhappy for some reason, the teachers should be just as concerned as you are: the mark of a good school is that its focus is always on the children. But they remain *your* children first and the final judgement is yours.

18. Talking Proper: Murder most vowel

If this seems an odd sort of topic to you, since children's speech is quite natural and not something to worry or pontificate about, then congratulations. You are laudably self-confident and come from a classless society. For most parents, life with young children is shot through with moments of alarm at the way they speak: expressions, accents, profanities, euphemisms all ringing alarm bells.

Some parents make major, and hilarious, drama out of it. One year there was a nice little sub-plot in that inimitable soap opera of British middle-class life, 'The Archers'. The appalling Jennifer Aldridge hires a girl from Birmingham as nanny to her small baby. Then she lies in bed fretting at her husband Brian about whether Dawn's robust Brummie accent is a drawback, and whether baby Alice, aged three months, might pick it up and start talking in a 'common' way. This is a great joke, considering that Jennifer herself has the most objectionable accent. She speaks in a sort of mincing, narrow-vowelled, fake upper-class simper. 'Ay don't want Alice to talk like a Brem-mie, Bry-un,' she says shudderingly. Brian, however, is asleep. He doesn't care. He knows perfectly well that as long as Alice has lots and lots of money and goes to a nice private school, it does not matter too much if her first baby words are 'Ey-oop, ah'm jiggered' or 'Okay, yah'.

It is a quintessentially British failing, placing people by their accents: but every nation has its version. You can make a Bostonian very uncomfortable by teaching his child a sharp Bronx twang, and a Parisian will flinch at broad Provençal expressions coming from his precious little Lycéen. Here, the truth of Shaw's *Pygmalion* holds only too good: an Englishman cannot open his mouth without making another Englishman despise him. Click, registers the mental computer, and up flashes the message. It might be harmless enough – 'She's Welsh . . . Irish . . . Scottish' – but it might equally say 'Vulgar' or 'Yokel' or 'Bleedin' toff'. How many social pitfalls lie ahead of your little ones? If Dawn from Brum teaches little Alice to say 'Beg pardon, but where's the toilet?' will she ever live it down at St Snobberina's Academy for the Socially Ambitious?

Teenagers know very well how you get placed by your accent. English public schoolboys will frequently be found slopping around saying 'Er, yeah, brill, magic, lads' in an accent never heard on sea or land (somewhere between Liverpool and California, with overtones of Eton), when they want to disguise themselves as democratic proles. For years I said 'Yup' instead of yes, because I was terrified that 'Yes' would come out as 'Ye-ahs' and everyone would guess I had been brought up in Embassies and Consulates instead of the accepted Sixties background of a cobbled street well north of Watford. Today in Britain the vogue for the young Royals has swung the pendulum back a bit, and many teenagers have no objection to sounding Sloaney and saying 'Yah, reahhly' a lot. Poor kids.

But we are not too concerned with them yet. What about the *little* children, ours? Is there any point trying to teach them to talk in the standard, 'correct' form? Is there a correct form, anyway? If you talk about BBC English do you mean Radio 1 ('Fa-yun-tastic! Yeah!'), Radio 2 ('Vis is Old Del 'ere, do vey mean us?'), Radio 3 ('Mozart's Pi-ar-no Con-*cher*-to'), or Radio 4 ('BBC Radio News at – six o'clock')? If a child comes home from a Norfolk school sneezing and saying 'Ow, this win'er weather, that hent noo fun' or from a Yorkshire one feeling 'Reet mardy', is that cause for panic or amusement?

The first thing to say is that all children are natural mimics. They try out everything they hear. My son, at barely two, could do a brilliant imitation of Mummy failing to start the Landrover: 'Eheu-eheu eheu. Eheu. Eheu-eheu. Oh soddy, soddy. Eheu-eheu VROOM!' The linguistic expert David Crystal, in his brilliant book *Listen to your Child*, quotes a little boy who kept saying 'Christ!' and when asked what it meant, said, 'It means there's no room in the car park.' Children will copy the speech mannerisms and general sound of anyone within earshot. They are also quite capable of being bilingual: not only between two complete languages, as often happens without trouble in a marriage of two nationalities, but between uses of the same language. Plenty of children talk in correct cut-glass accents at home and the classroom, and in broad regional ones in the school playground. They occasionally muddle the languages and alarm their parents, but on picking up the message of horror from a parent who has heard them say 'Push off, yer daft git' or a schoolmate who has heard them say 'frightfully sorry', they adapt rapidly. The only thing which Jennifer and Bry-un ought to consider is that Alice really will grow up with Dawn's accent if they intend to spend very little time with her themselves. Example is all.

Prithee Mama,
kill the fatted fishfingers
thy beloved child has
come
home

The third point, and by far the most important, is that children love language. All of it, without prejudice. Words are a new country to the growing baby, and he revels in it: try to teach a baby to say 'cat' for too long and he may lose interest: try 'Rimsky-Korsakov' or 'Supercalifragilisticexpialidocious' and he will bravely have a go, and laugh. A two-year-old loves rhymes and easy puns, a three-year-old is enchanted to learn a few foreign words. (English children say 'Mercy Boko' for thank-you, with the same delight that French children say 'Sankyoo'.) They play with words: a four-year-old boy (not mine) once pointed at the sea and said 'Fish and ships!' before doubling up. My own daughter said 'Granny's got over her *pneu*monia, now she's an old moanier!' It is part of the natural delight in language, the highest of human achievements. When a five- or six-year-old comes home from school laughing, it is to tell you some terrible, terrible joke: the odds are that it will be based on verbal ambiguity or deceitful use of language:

'What animal can jump higher than a house? Any animal, houses can't jump.'

'What sort of animal tells the time? A watch dog!'

'What did the one wall say to the other wall? See you on the corner!'

'Knock Knock! Who's there? Teresa! Teresa who? Trees are usually quite tall.'

'Knock Knock! Who's there? Banana. Knock knock! Who's there? Banana. Knock knock! Who's there? Banana. Knock knock! Who's there? Orange! Orange who? Aren'ja glad it's not another banana?'

Well, you know the genre. They are a tremendous sign of progress. You should cherish them.

Children also need to be exposed to wonderful language: to ceremonial, grand, beautiful words. It is a great shame that we talk down to them so much, in books and prayers and poems for children. A six-year-old has the capacity to be thrilled by the language of the King James Bible, by snatches of Milton. C S Lewis wrote that the line

'Thrones, Dominations, Princedoms, Virtues, Powers'

once kept him happy – in an unhappy childhood – for a week. It need not be archaic language, but it should be rich. Read them books with some style about them, and don't be afraid of the long descriptive passages unless the children obviously are restless. Try old-fashioned books sometimes, or fairytales told in the old grand manner. Turns of phrase, fine words, will creep into their vocabulary painlessly and be brought out at

131

times of need. I have never forgotten the night when my daughter, still almost a baby, suffered a night terror and my son of five came up and put his hand on her shoulder and said, earnestly, looking her in the eye: 'Rose, do not fear. No stranger comes.' Where he picked up that lovely iambic sentence, that dramatic inversion – from what story or rhyme, I do not know. But he *needed* it, the specialness and poetry of it, to meet the emotion of the moment. On another occasion Rose sang a song to us on the boat, mingling every element of grandeur that she could find from song or carol or story:

> 'The glory of the West in the sunlight
> In the ranks of South Australia,
> Spanish ships sailing the East Coast
> Going West
> Sailors sailing, sailing to harbour
> In the ranks of Beth-le-hem!'

I am not fondly bragging. Every child, every single child, has such moments of elevated imagination, and grabs words from its experience to express them. If they have heard words like glory and miracle, majesty, ancient, echo, despair, rejoicing, they will use them. Wrongly, on occasion: but with great gusto and appreciation. If all they ever hear is a banal vocabulary of 'nice, super, brilliant, great, good boy, uh-uh, naughty, bad, eat your supper', they will be impoverished. Language is communication, but it is also music. Find them decent books, not the zap-pow macho nonsense of *Masters of the Universe*, nor the pretty-pretty blandness of money-spinning fairies and little ponies whose spiritual home is on duvet covers rather than bookshelves. Buy or borrow classics, old and new. Read Erik the Viking and E Nesbit, Narnia books and *Linnets and Valerians*, Margaret Mahy and the better books of Roald Dahl. Take them to the theatre if you can, or let them watch classic children's serials on television as well as (or instead of) the inverted snob, yobbish 'Yer, fantastic, loadsamoney, motormouth' kind. Declaim from an old-fashioned poetry book. Though less intense than Lewis, I remember walking around for months as a small child saying to myself, 'The Assyrian came down like a wolf on the fold, and his cohorts were gleaming in purple and gold.' I did not know what an Assyrian was, or a cohort, but I knew they must be grand. Even if you are not a great reader yourself, you can give your child an inheritance of dazzling words, dazzlingly deployed. And – here you may think I enter the realms of fantastic optimism – it lessens the need for, and the frequency of, swearwords. A child who is equipped to call you (as I once called my brother) a 'Monster of iniquity', is marginally less likely to call you a bloody old cow.

And are you really going to ruin this joyful initiation into language by nagging your offspring about pronunciation, or grammar, or 'common' expressions? Don't do it. Don't let Daddy or Granny do it. Or at least, not until they reach their teens. The only words worth fighting for, in that depressing way, are 'Please' and 'Thank you': let the rest run free.

There is only one certain way to give a child the gift of clear and acceptable speech, and that is to converse freely and constantly yourself. Don't correct, just discreetly show the way. It is the same principle that you used in early talking lessons: if he says 'I saw a mixmenter' you said 'Oh, where was the cement-mixer? Was it in the road?' and got the message through that way, without reproof. Children can take hints. The same applies at this older stage, even more so because their feelings are so easily hurt. If you jump on every incorrect or unfortunate expression, they will give up trying new words on you at all. If you care about accent and pronunciation, then watch your own grammar and vowels (and be sure to say interesting things in your nice voice, and tell good stories). Cut down on slang if you must, but more importantly cut down on boring, meaning-less phrases like 'Know what I mean' and 'This is it'. If you hear your child keep saying 'Well, this is it', you know where it probably came from as surely as you know why he shouted 'Oh, shit!' when his Lego failed to hold together.

But vocabulary, communication, and enjoyment are all more important than accent or correctness any day. If you are really worried that your child at six or seven doesn't express himself clearly, there are games that you can play, without pressure.

One is storytelling, where each member of the family stops a story in the middle and the next carries on. Another very good one is to get on the floor with some Lego bricks, giving him an identical selection, put a visual barrier between you (like an armchair) then ask him to make a building and tell you exactly what he is doing so you can build an identical one. It helps the child to use spatial words, describe colours and shapes, and sort out concepts like 'opposite' and 'sideways'. And the huge advantage of it is that if he isn't very good at it, it is *you* who fail – your building is the wonky one. It may even produce a new word for the language: after a session of this, a friend's mildly handicapped girl rose to peer over the sofa at the mess her mother had made under her directions. 'That,' she said, 'is not a house like mine. It is a scrambunctious mess.' Not bad.

19. Whoopee: Treats and trips

Taking children on formal, old-fashioned treats becomes suddenly more rewarding after the age of four. Before that, their tolerance is short and you find yourself spending many a miserable hour at some fair which none of you is enjoying, or queuing in the rain for something the child would as soon as not bother with. Early treats have to be close by, and brief in duration, or else something the adults so long to do that a bit of infantile whining does not ruin them.

Now, however, with four-to-eights, it becomes the shared fun you always hoped it would be. They have learned to look forward in anticipation, to be a bit patient in the car on the way, and to enjoy the thrill of collecting tiny souvenirs. They can, at small events, be trusted to go and buy their own ice creams (with you, needless to say, watching closely all the time) and show other small signs of independence.

The same rules apply as before: keep an eye out for signs saying TOILET even when nobody wants one yet, take a change of tracksuit in case of mud, rain, or accidents, and take your own fruit juice cartons and biscuits in case there is nothing to refresh the inner child. Prepare the ground, research the nature of the treat, and take advice more readily from fellow-parents than from Tourist Board brochures. One tip: now that children are well and truly beyond the age of reins and harnesses – and even strict hand-holding – if you go to crowded places try to dress each child of a pair in one identical garment – yellow sweater, the same anoraks, plaid trousers, whatever. That way, if you lose one you can brandish the remaining child of the pair and say to every passer-by, 'Have you seen another one wearing one of these?' It is amazing how effective this can be. If you lose both, you are really not concentrating and your only hope is to take a granny with you next time. Grannies are very vigilant. Unless, that is, they are the sort who wander off and get lost themselves.

Here are some good treats:

Theatre trips Of all the set-piece treats, these are the most worthwhile. Children are actors. Watch any toddler pull a pair of knickers on to its head and stare admiringly into the mirror. Hats and turbans are usually the first step to dressing up, because a hat is the quickest way to change your identity. The next thing is shoes. Beryl Reid says that the way she gets into a new part is to get the shoes right, and everything else follows. Any three-year-old clumping around in Daddy's wellington boots could tell you that. It is a great day for a child, when it grows tall enough to put its parents' wellingtons on without suffering too much discomfort around the crotch.

Next come jackets, cardigans, shawls, tablecloths, pillowcases and masks. After that, if you have any sense, you provide a proper dressing-up box, generously filled with a jumble of old clothes (shirts with frayed collars, battered rain hats, and those little sequinned tops Mummy wore in her disco days, before breastfeeding modified her own little top beyond repair). I believe there are families who manage without a dressing-up box, but I cannot see how. In our house, such a box is the only hope of stopping the children from borrowing every other garment in the house. The mystery remains why they will not dress themselves for school, when they are so quick and skilful at deciding to 'do a play' by donning military jackets, plastic fireman's helmets, ragged pirate trousers, thick face-paint and Hawaiian shirts with bits cut out for the last patchwork quilt. But I digress.

Drama is not a luxury, it is an instinct. It needs feeding with a few professional or good amateur productions, treats which inspire hours of games and performances on toy theatres. Living in deep Suffolk, we are not frequent theatregoers with the children: if we were Londoners, they would no doubt be whooshed from marionette-show to Molecule Theatre and virtually live on the South Bank. As it is, we might choose one or two really good children's plays per year, and otherwise rely on the pantomime to invigorate them every Christmas.

Never despise pantomime. A good one is a perfect introduction to the joys of theatre: spectacle, involvement, and the willing but knowing suspension of disbelief. You laugh, you tremble, you sympathize, and you wonder how they got the Giant Pumpkin on to the stage. It is grand opera, it is Shakespeare, it is circus, it is Greek tragedy, all reduced to childlike proportion. Sometimes, I grant you, it is reduced too far: even infants can have their intelligence insulted by some productions, and as David Holman's plays have proved, seven-year-olds are capable of taking in some powerful, non-comic drama as well. But on the whole, pantomime or a children's comedy is not a bad beginning.

- *Finding one* It is very unwise to take a child to its very first theatrical production without finding out all you can about it. Is it a noisy showbiz production full of rock 'n roll and smutty jokes? How long is it? Is there a story you could explain beforehand? Reviews help a bit, but above all word-of-mouth recommendation is the key. The best bet may be a small local amateur production in a church hall. Small children get so fascinated with the whole idea of curtains going up and down and people being disguised, that they quite enjoy the fact that they can see the stage-hand's arm doing the winding, and that the villain is clearly the plumber who unblocked your drains last week. Also, church halls are less frightening for the timid.

- *Preparing children* They ought to be told several things. Firstly, that the lights will go out in the auditorium. Secondly, that all the villains on stage are just people's Daddies, dressed up for a laugh. Thirdly, that you have to sit quietly and watch, or whisper very quietly, or go out. I neglected all this, and was rewarded with a moment of blind terror from my daughter the moment the lights went out, shrieks, kicks, hysteria and profound embarrassment. Since I had also neglected the rule of one-adult-per-young-child on the first visit, I was in the embarrassing position of trying to carry a yelling, terrified child along a row of seats while another hysterical, screaming child behind me begged to be allowed to stay and watch, and me to stay with him. The actors on stage struggled on, valiantly, as I was dragged up and down the aisle by demented infants. It could all have been avoided, with a moment's thought.

The next time we tried this phobic child in a theatre – at her own request – I took an emergency Granny in the party to stay with the older one and his friends. There were smiles and confident announcements that she wouldn't be afraid. Curtain up, pretty dancing-girls, smiles. Then BANG! The Demon King appeared in red tights and orange smoke, going HAAHAHAAHAHAHAHAHA! I fled up the aisle (we had booked end seats, suspecting trouble) like an out-of-control bagpiper, with a wailing bundle under my arm. In the foyer, we reconsidered our position. Ten minutes later, we progressed to peering round the door at the back of the theatre. Later still, we resumed our seats. Well, my seat: she clung to me until her confidence returned. Unfortunately, it returned so thoroughly that by the second half she was standing on her seat shoeless, shrieking 'PISS OFF, DEMON!' Oh, the shame.

But it was worth it. The two of them acted out plays and pantomimes together for months, learning essential lessons: that things are not always as they seem, that sometimes it helps to shout and express your feelings, that roles can be changed, pretences made and conflicts played out to a satisfactory conclusion. And that all of us, at least in our mirrors privately, have the right to be the heroes and beauties who star in our own wonderful stories.

Cinemas Most of the same cautions apply. Cinema is less intense than theatre, more so than television: it is still worthwhile. Films, however, need even more careful vetting than theatrical performances: some of those produced for 'children' – a wide, sloppy category – and bearing a U certificate are really not fit for the eyes of under-thirteens. The worst fault of films, as far as little children are concerned, is their tiresome habit of allusiveness: they assume their audience to be totally plugged in to a particular stream of Americanized schoolkid culture and to understand all its references. A European six-year-old may be utterly baffled by most of it. The old Disney standards are always a success; Superman comes into his own at ages over seven, in my view, as do the Spielberg blockbusters.

One warning: cinema managements are very insensitive about young children, and often put on tacky trailers for '18' films, and disproportionately violent and frightening 'B' features with a soppy, gentle main film. The experience of trying to calm down three petrified little boys of five faced with *Peter and the Wolf* (big yellow teeth) when we had come to see *101 Dalmatians* and only prepared them for Cruella de Ville is something I would not wish to repeat. Ring up and ask.

Museums Have suddenly discovered young children in the last decade. Gone are the rows of dull glass cases and the hushed, scholarly atmosphere: they are becoming almost too good, full of moving dinosaurs and feely-boxes and machines you can wind up yourself. The only trouble is that if you have a rather hushed scholarly sort of child, who actually enjoys staring into glass cases at the teeth of pterodactyls, he may get frustrated. In the City Museum in York, we went to look specifically at suits of armour, and found that it was compulsory to walk round on a pre-set track, past all the reproductions of old shops, doll's houses, and everything else before we could get to them. It did nothing for anyone's temper.

The most successful sort of museums, which made our children very satisfactorily into addicts, are local ones: either humble little displays you can explain at leisure ('Those coins were dropped a thousand years ago, and have just been dug up. Vikings used them. What do you think they bought?'), or else the grander 'Heritage Centres' with displays which take you into the middle of a nineteenth-century lighthouse, or let you sit in the driving-seat of a tram. Never assume that children will be bored by a very straightforward museum: I once took mine into Norwich Castle Museum for no other reason than to get out of the sluicing Norwich rain, and we spent two hours communing with stuffed animals and spelling out the labels on mummy-cases. An extra frisson was added by the underfloor heating grilles, on which a little girl may stand and see her skirt blow up around her waist like Marilyn Monroe.

Museums can give children a very good graphic skeleton of history. In Portsmouth one day we saw the ships *Mary Rose* (16th century), HMS *Victory* (18th) and HMS *Warrior* (Victorian). Later we saw a Viking ship of the 11th century, in reproduction. From that day to this, when Nicholas wants to put something in perspective he says, 'Is that when *Mary Rose* was sailing? Or later? Before *Victory*, though?' All history is conveniently punctuated by ships changing shapes. You can do the same with castles, architecture, industrial inventions, anything.

Art Galleries Again, surprisingly successful. Young children merely roam around, and should not be dragged to look at painters in a systematic way, or even to learn their names unless they ask. From seven years old upwards, you can play the game Christina Hardyment describes in her European grand tour with her children: she let them each choose a postcard of a painting at the desk, then they had to hare off and find the original and lead her to it. Children should be told not to run in galleries, and not to chatter about anything except the exhibits: beyond that, any attempt to curb their enthusiasm or hush their voices is probably doomed. Smile a lot at the attendants. Most are quite understanding, especially if children are really looking at the pictures: 'Look! He's got a lion on his foot! It might bite him! Specially with no clothes on!'

Theme Parks We need them, because of the decline of the funfair. Once – and still, in a few places – there were steam funfairs, paradises of gleaming brass machinery, gentle and beautiful artwork, flowers and gilding and baroque flourishes to sail past mounted on your pole horse or steam-yacht. Modern funfairs are, on the whole, rackety, crudely coloured, violent in tone and often unsafe in fact (the exceptions all seem to be in Holland). They are geared to teenagers, not children. So American-style theme parks are stepping in, with wonderful fantasy rides, friendly furry bears that wander about waving aimlessly at everyone, nice little railways, ample lavatories, and strict, strict regulations. Also, you can often ride on everything for the price of the entry ticket, which defuses the financial tension of parents. For a big day out, they are matchless. But they do cloy very quickly. One outing per summer is probably enough.

Steam Fairs, Horse Shows, County Fairs and others All have their own local flavour. These events – rather nightmarish with toddlers – evolve into pleasant days out with older children. Especially if you have no overwhelming need to find any particular engine or horse, but meander along and let them lead the way. Choose the event depending on whether your children like steam-engines or Shire horses best: the adjacent stalls, roundabouts, charity markets, bouncy castle, and such, will be much the same. Any event run by the local Rotary Club is bound to have decent Portaloos. Or so I have always found.

Battles Various societies of obsessives are in the habit of re-enacting historical battles – Civil War, medieval jousts, Viking scuffles. Even the gentlest of children seem to adore these. Just remember two things: don't sit too near the ropes, because not all of them are very good at hanging on to their flails, axe-heads, or whatever; and be resigned to a houseful of mayhem for weeks afterwards. Take the chance to impart some history, even if (like me) you have to read it up surreptitiously yourself from a Children's Encyclopaedia beforehand.

Holidays

Again, holiday travel becomes suddenly far easier after four. Children who can crayon, look at books or listen to Walkmans are manageable in cars and trains and aeroplanes. What is the best diversion depends entirely on your child, and I would not dream of prescribing them too closely: small toys help, board games for some, little prisms to distort the world for others, pencils and paper for all. The best toy for a travelling child is another child the same age: pooling families can make things far more pleasant. The only other bit of advice I would presume to give is *don't take too much*. I am a light packer, and yet I have never, ever, used all the children's clothes I packed. Not once. Pack the minimum, then take two things per child out. As long as one of them is not Teddy.

What is worth thinking about is: *what kind of holiday*? If you are personally, as adults, utterly set on Turkey, or Venice, or a villa in Spain, or a flotilla cruise in the Mediterranean, then your own problem is how to fit the children into it, or how to leave them at home for a fortnight and compensate later with treats. Children over five can quite well be fitted into exotic adult holidays. But it takes a lot of work, and for the children the rewards may be dubious, and not enough to repay the air fares. Beautiful Greek beaches may actually be made of gritty gravel and poisonous sea-urchins, and hotels with romantic balconies may be death traps for bored clambering children. Even cruise ships and flotilla yachts can feel like prison hulks to a child who prefers kicking footballs to any other of life's joys.

Also, think of what children actually say about past holidays. 'What did you enjoy most?' we ask. And they reply, 'Ooh, the best bit was when Daddy changed the tyre on the car going to the airport, and we helped with the jack.' After trying out various types of holiday and canvassing friends, I have come to the startling conclusion that small children actually prefer rather spartan holidays, and that it is a shame that the crazy economics of Western tourism often make it cheaper for families to go on a package to a Spanish hotel, than to wander about exploring their own country's odd edges. Cheaper or not, it is certainly easier to arrange: just put yourself in the hands of a travel agent, opt for the page you like best in the brochure, and everything else should happen predictably. There will be a bus at the airport, a courier to see you through customs, and an English-speaking hotel manager who understands what cornflakes are. And if these things fail to materialize, you can always complain to the travel agent. Going on holiday has been turned into a very passive business: not so much holidaymaking as holiday-receiving.

How different to the holidays of remembered childhood! In the days before Gatwick and Luton and the package trade, we used to see our parents poring over train timetables, arguing about ferries, reading guidebooks, and even *looking at maps*. A quick straw poll taken by a travel journalist revealed that, shown a map, only one in fifty British tourists in Spain, and only slightly more Germans, could accurately point at which section of coast they were staying on. The old-fashioned bucket-and-spade and boarding-house holiday is declining, because adults like it that way: all they want from a holiday is a bit of sun, a bit of swimming, someone else to cook the food, and a disco in the evening. They don't want a challenge, or an education. And if anything goes wrong, they don't get excited and write about it in their journals, they grumble to officials. That is what makes a tourist instead of a real traveller.

But what about the children? They need challenges and broader horizons. Doing the best from the child's point of view doesn't necessarily mean taking him to the biggest and best theme park, or on a plane to the Mediterranean. Children are not as sun-struck as adults, nor as blasé about entertainment. They like simple things, like jumping in puddles and watching waves crash over a seaside promenade in a gale. They are often more excited by the swooshing northern tides, ('Oh Mummy, is that God doing that?' asked my son the first time a wave filled up his ditch) than by the gritty tideless beaches of the south, where giant vacuum cleaners have to clear the debris daily, and you can hardly run around without falling over torpid, oily adult bodies.

In any case, for a young child three-quarters of the pleasure of a holiday is having the constant company of both parents. In modern life, children already miss out on one huge, vital chunk of experience because they so rarely see their parents working. The adult world, the adult mind, is a mystery. They may watch their mother overcoming everyday problems, and doing routine jobs at home, but they rarely see their father weaving a carpet or mending a plough for his living. Fathers

143

tend to be shut away in mysterious offices and factories, doing incomprehensible things. So, more and more, do mothers.

So holidays are doubly important, and in the past the old style of do-it-yourself holiday used to be a chance to watch your parents overcoming real problems – tents that won't go up, or trains that leave you stranded. It gave you, the child, the chance to act as a partner in resolving the crises. A mother interviewed by Gwenda Cornell, in *Cruising with Children*, said:

> 'At sea, my son saw his father Bruce actually working, coping with problems under stress, as when gear broke in heavy weather. Before we went, he only used to see his father for a short time each day, tired after a day's work. Now Jeff has more respect for his father and a stronger relationship.'

Not everyone is going to embark on a life-or-death venture like transatlantic sailing with children, but the principle holds good. The times my children talk about are when we all trudged across a bleak Irish beach carrying a little camp-stove to make tea; when we hired a horse-drawn caravan with extremely basic, not to say grim, facilities and plank beds and trekked across Norfolk for three days, staking the horse out each night; when we climbed a hill together to a castle, and hid in the ruins from the British rain; or when we went on the Norfolk Broads in a dreadful houseboat and got blown into the rushes by gale-force winds. They have few memories of the packaged, group things we have done: just a dim sense of Mummy and Daddy waiting crossly and helplessly for the airport coach, along with fifty other herded passengers at midnight in a foreign airport. Parents passive, parents dependent on a bossy lady courier, parents made to sit in a row until the bus came, and hand over their passports: is that a holiday memory to enrich the rest of the year?

Children can have wonderful holidays abroad; some packages leave at least a bit of liberty and self-determination for parents. But if you are restricted by money to a hired caravan, or a tent on a windswept camping-site nearer home, take heart. Children will get as much out of it, or more: discovering starfish and rabbit-holes at your side, exploring local museums, learning the folk tales of the region, making maps and working out the next day's walk. And you will have real memories to share, of a holiday that may have been uncomfortable at times, but was like nobody else's: your private family adventure.

The only problem is that after one of these pioneering, gritty, sandy, independent traditional holidays with young children, the parents usually feel like having another one to get over it. Round it off with a long weekend *à deux* in Paris, perhaps? Let the little ones stay at home with Granny, renewing joyful acquaintance with their half-forgotten toys, while the photos get developed and the soggy tent and sleeping-bags dry out slowly in the garage, and Mummy and Daddy eat moules in Montmartre. Well, that is what we dream of, anyway. It hasn't happened yet.

20. On the Mend: Hospitals and hacking coughs

If you want to be convinced of the frailty of the human body, try sitting in a Casualty department for an hour on a fine Sunday evening. Kids hobble by on crutches, still wearing the dayglo shorts and elbow-pads which indicate that half an hour ago they were kings of the world on their skateboards. Glum-looking toddlers sit on their mothers' knees, one wrist suspiciously chubbier than the other. Adults sit clutching various wounds inflicted by lawnmowers, dogs, and other acts of God. There may be a teenager in a netball-skirt, hopping around explaining to her father how she only just missed the equalizer; and at least one child with its finger stuck in some treacherous domestic utensil, or wrapped hastily and bloodily up in something that looks very like its baby brother's vest. They all sit there, obedient and unnerved, waiting to be given a hospital number and turned into patients with neat white proper bandages on; the adults occasionally prowl hopelessly in search of something to read other than the usual hospital issue of a 10-year-old copy of *Reveille* and half a knitting-pattern. Sometimes – not nearly often enough – a brisk nurse whisks out and calls somebody's name.

The Casualty waiting room is a unique place, even within the hospital. Medical clinics have a completely different feeling because most of their customers have had an appointment for weeks, and known about their problem for longer. They are acclimatized. They have bought magazines to read, or knitting; the children have been carefully prepared for the experience with cosy little books called *Mary's Happy Hospital Visit*, or *Percy Pig Gets His Hernia Done*. Everyone has had time to practise having a bright, sensible attitude to it all. There have been 'counselling', and family conferences.

In real emergencies, where life and death are at stake and

will be decided in moments, everything is different again: dramatic and desperate, with trolleys and rushing and fears of the worst. When you are fearing the worst you don't feel boredom or embarrassment: it is only in Casualty waiting rooms that adults and children alike have this curiously forlorn look, like a row of landed and stunned codfish. Minutes ago they were larking around in the sun, now here they are feeling let down and foolish, facing up to the fact that a split-second misjudgement may mean weeks in itchy plaster. Above all, the parents of injured children are either pointlessly blaming themselves in silence, or else tearfully assuring everyone else in the waiting room that it was a very well-built tree house really, who could ever have known he'd try handstands on the safety rail . . .

Which is where we come in. Where, to be precise, my four-year-old daughter and I came in, through the electric double doors of Heath Road Hospital Accident and Emergency Department in Ipswich. After a weekend of visits to the GP ('Probably a sprain, hard to tell') we had been advised to get her wrist X-rayed as it wasn't improving and might, just might, be broken. We felt pretty silly: having in the previous year sailed 1,700 miles and climbed forty-five harbour ladders in various states of disrepair, without a scratch, the child had actually slipped on the patent non-slip surface at the local swimming pool. Still, it could happen to anyone: once, it happened to a friend of mine twice within ten minutes, when her two children broke one leg each.

It might happen to you next. In order that you may face the experience with more dignity, calm and efficiency than I managed, here are some hard-won facts of Casualty life. They are gleaned from bitter experience and muttered questions to other parents.

Rule One is that you should never approach a hospital, if you can help it, without a personal comforts bag. If there is any time at all, if it is not a desperate matter of unconsciousness or haemorrhage, allow yourself five minutes to think and pack a few things. Do not be a wally, like I was, and dash off on a forty-minute drive with the child shoeless and coatless, no handbag, money, tissues, drinks of water or reading matter. You will have plenty of time to ponder your shortcomings as you sit on a vinyl bench in Casualty awaiting your turn. By great good luck, my car is an ambulant rubbish tip, so there was an ancient copy of *Alice through the Looking-Glass* stuck behind one of the seats. Without it, things would have been pretty unbearable for Rose (and me) during the hour's wait outside, the fifteen minutes outside X-ray, another twenty minutes waiting for the doctor to see the X-ray, and sundry other waits. In the end we got all the way to the White Knight before actually finding out what was wrong with her arm.

I was deeply admiring of a woman who had come in with a black-eyed, blood-caked, limping nine-year-old but had some-how managed also to bring a carton of apple juice, a pile of comics, her knitting, and his Sony Walkman with a supply of story tapes. 'Well, it's our third time in Casualty,' she said. 'Or is it our fourth? He's ever so brave on his BMX bike. Just like his dad. His dad's broken both legs, on the speedway. We like this hospital, they're ever so nice.' Experience tells.

Rule Two concerns the way you talk to the child. Once you are in a hospital, *do not* promise anything except that 'the doctor will try to help you get better' and 'Mummy/Daddy won't leave you'. The second promise is more or less safe to make: few hospital procedures involving a conscious child now exclude parents. It has been a hard-won right, as any Sixties mother will tell you: there was a time when you handed your child over at the door of the X-ray unit, into a world of strangers with strange machines; and a time even more recently when children's ward sisters actually discouraged visitors for in-pati-ents because it 'unsettled' them. Today you can say 'Mummy will stay close' and mean it. However, do not start making rash promises like, 'Of course, the doctor won't hurt your sore place, he'll just look at it' (he might hurt it: he might have to), or 'No, I'm sure you won't have to have a horrid plaster on'. Above all, don't say 'I'm sure we'll be home in time for *Thundercats*.' You won't.

Continuing our tale: we had a check by a charming woman

doctor, and a session in an X-ray unit which gave Rose a skeleton badge saying 'I'M AN X-RAY FILM STAR'. So I got overconfident and began breaking Rule Two. 'We'll be home soon, and won't Daddy be pleased to see your badge?' Another doctor materialized from behind a curtain. 'I'm afraid it's a double greenstick fracture.' Right, no problem, I had explained to Rose all about plaster in the car. She was quite looking forward to it. 'Oh yes, I know about greensticks. Isn't that the plaster room over there? How long do you – ' 'We're admitting her to the ward,' he said. 'Now.'

Collapse of Mummy, panic inadequately veiled in baffled smile: the Cleveland case has made paranoiacs of us all. Did they think I might break her other arm, were social workers lurking behind every pillar? Here we were in their power, away from the street door of the clinic, on the hospital side of the big internal doors. Around us were rows of crutches and bandages and hurrying porters and doctors; we were through the looking-glass like Alice, and anything could happen. I had discovered:

Rule Three: Never assume you're just an out-patient. The doctor rapidly explained his reasoning: because it was evening, and they might have to manipulate the arm under general anaesthetic, they thought Rose would be better off on the ward. Like a police suspect I felt entitled to one phone call: I summoned up clothes, money, a comb and toothbrush for both of us, and the all-important Jingle the bear. My husband was at home with our other child and a neighbour was around to take over while he drove up; I shuddered to think that, if Paul had been away, I might well have dropped Nicholas casually on a neighbour without giving her so much as a key to our house for getting pyjamas and teddies. So:

Rule Four: Use some of that waiting-time in thinking out contingency plans in case you have to stay away for the night. It is a useful mental exercise, even though rarely needed. (Do not, however, emulate my friend Victoria who plans out in detail an entire lifetime of support for a permanent invalid every time

149

one of the family sneezes. She reads the Health Page of the *Independent* too closely, I always think.)

We sat for a while, Rose and I, in that bewildering corridor between two worlds. We were neither in-patients nor out-patients, not free to leave but not yet having a place of our own inside the hospital. 'We're sort of lost, aren't we, Mummy?' she said, and I agreed that we were, but at least we were lost together. Then they took us to the ward and it was – as most children's wards are, thanks to years of reformers and fundraisers – delightful. Once surrounded by nurses in Mister Men aprons, dangling mobiles, toys and children's paintings, we felt less lost. Rose's only crisis of confidence occurred when a sister came to explain the procedures for the operating theatre with the help of a book about Herbie the Hedgehog who lost his spines and put on some Magic Ointment provided by the fairies. Rose took one look at the book and began to weep. 'I'm not up to strange hedgehogs,' she said, quite understandably. So:

Rule Five: Find out all you can about each step yourself, and interpret it yourself to your own child. Especially to an exhausted four-year-old. Older children might want to discuss their case with the doctor, and have a perfect right to. But if you think back to how you felt in the labour ward, and how glad you were to have a husband or supporter around to represent you to the white-coated figures of authority, you will get an inkling of how your child feels.

They have beds for parents, at Heath Road; if your hospital doesn't, fund-raise and campaign now. When the patient had been wheeled into the operating theatre three-quarters asleep, and wheeled out fast asleep, I got six hours in a quiet bedroom myself, and was back on the ward in time for Rose to wake, yawn, and roll comfortably off her bed straight on to my knee. By great good fortune, two hours later we were sent home, and three weeks later the plaster came off. It is preserved as a grisly relic in a plastic bag with her whole class's sprawling signatures all over it. 'On the whole,' as she observed, 'it's not too bad breaking your arm, is it?' By some strange paradox, small children are more fragile than us, but also a great deal tougher.

It isn't her that still has nightmares about it all. It's me.

Since then I have talked to many other parents with longer, less banal experiences of hospital, either through children's illness or accident. They all agree that the rules for the child's welfare are obvious: be calm, be competent, talk the case over privately with the doctors (whether they like it or not), interpret it your own way to the child, and – if at all possible – be *there*. However, if you can't, be content with your best. I once spent twenty-four hours on a children's ward for a journalistic assignment, and grew furious about one little boy of seven with a leg in traction, who cried for his Mummy and stared sadly at every new visitor to the ward. From 7 a.m. to 11 a.m. I cursed this heartless bitch who couldn't even be bothered to stay with her own child. At eleven she arrived, and I spent the next four hours silently cursing myself instead. She had, so she told me in a brief moment in the Ladies, come via three different buses, leaving children of one, two, and four at home with a neighbour; her husband had left her the year before, and the boy's road accident had forced her to give up her job and go on social security which barely paid for food. But she had arrived with a cheerful little picnic, home-made toys, and pictures from the small siblings, and sat chattering and singing to her little boy for several hours, as if she hadn't a care in the world. She taught me the other rule: that your best is good enough, and guilty weeping over your child won't help.

But there is one more hospital rule: even if you stay all day and night, get out of it sometimes. Children do sleep: nurses can be trusted to be kind to them if they wake. It is hot and enervating in hospital, overlit and undomestic. It makes you feel unreal and institutionalized and helpless to control your own life. In order to bring a breath of fresh normal air in to your child, you have to get outside the building once a day, even if only to walk round the block in the rain and buy a magazine from a corner newsagent and discuss something bland with him, like the weather.

Most childhood illness, of course, does not involve a hospital at all. It involves a box of tissues, a jar of Vick, and a lot of endurance. Turn to your medical dictionary for advice (and a quite unnecessary fright or two), but take my word for it that children's illnesses generally follow a set pattern:

Act I Appalling behaviour Suddenly he or she is two years younger, six times whinier, and not at all nice to know. You get irritated, threaten to dock pocket money and send him to bed. Suddenly the child says he wouldn't mind, actually, going to bed. He develops a symptom: under six or seven it almost inevitably takes the form of vomiting all over the place, over that age it presents itself as 'a headache'. So, you are precipitated, anxious and loving, into

Act II Nursing Apart from your dreadful guilt at having been so cross with him earlier, this is the easy bit. You get the doctor, or go to the surgery, and the doctor does the usual checks for meningitis or inflamed ears, then looks reassuring and tells you it is 'a virus that's going round'. Either you get an antibiotic syrup or you don't. The child has some mild painkiller and goes to sleep, waking four or five times in a sweat but otherwise improving slowly. Sometimes the most sensible thing is to share a big bed with him by yourself, with bucket and towel at hand. Maybe some vivid spots come out and it is chicken-pox; maybe bits swell, and it is mumps. Then comes the very worst bit:

Act III Convalescence School or playgroup is out of the question, but so is bed. No diversion lasts more than five minutes. Television or videos help immensely, especially for a child who is normally rationed; but your patience is tried as at no other time. Especially as you have now caught the bug yourself and feel like death.

This last disaster is worth examining. The nursing of children is a subject covered in many books, but nobody gives much thought to the problem of what, precisely, is supposed to happen in the well-regulated household when Mummy Gets the Mumps. Yet looking after small children, especially once they mix freely with other small children, is like trekking across some fever-laden swamp. The bugs they bring home often turn out to be mild for them, but extremely nasty for adults. The little ones sniffle and recover; *we* are left reeling with flu for days. They get a briefly swollen face, and sit around eating ice cream and watching 'Popeye'; *we* catch mumps and go around feeling as if we had been sandbagged and left for dead. *They* get mild chicken-pox, *we* get appalling shingles. And so on. They, after all, are new and strong. We are old and extremely battered. Well, I am, anyway.

Working – or part-time working – mothers get a particularly raw deal. There is an all-too-familiar cycle of family illness in which first the children get ill (one by one, naturally), thus disrupting the household; then Mummy gets ill, and when she recovers the nanny or babysitter has got it. Everyone sits around gloomy, convalescent, and in their boss's bad books, brooding on the inevitable fact that by this time next week Daddy in turn will be swollen up like the Phantom of the Opera, and will spend several days living from one dose of Panadol to the next and evading his responsibilities.

Children, quite rightly, get looked after when they are ill. If they want to sleep all day, they can. Drinks of water are available day and night for no more effort than a feeble cry. Diet is supervised. Gentle cooling baths are given. No wonder they get better so fast. But parents have nobody to tend them, especially mummies at home. Her illness follows a far less satisfying pattern than her children's. About six, feeling even more trembly and exhausted than usual, off she goes to the doctor croaking, 'I think I've got this . . . aah, no darling, don't break the doctor's stethoscope – this virus thing the children had . . . my head is splitting – I think I've got a temperature, only the dog ate the digital thermometer thing – no, sweetheart, we'll get an ice cream when we go home . . . don't hit the baby . . .' The doctor replies, 'Ah, hmmm, yes, nothing too serious here Mrs Ah . . . couple of days' rest should do the trick. Just stay indoors and take things easy.'

Easy? The doctor clearly suspects that, left to herself, the poor woman would whip up a gross of jam tarts for the local bazaar and swim forty lengths of the swimming baths. He reckons she could ease up her schedule nicely just by putting off the jobs of hand-starching the pelmets and running up a set of new duvet covers. He does not realize that with a houseful of children, some probably pre-school, time is not something you have much choice about. Very few of the routine jobs are unnecessary. Mummy has probably spent the last eighteen months trying to finish the same paperback novel.

Even if she 'takes it easy' to the maximum degree, children still need dressing, washing, feeding, amusing, taking to school or supervising, and preventing from climbing out of the windows. They want their questions answered. They want to know how space rockets fly. They need walks in the fresh air, or they get fractious – what does the doctor mean 'stay indoors'? Suppose you live in a flat and can't send them safely into the garden?

Then they need a bath, and something clean to wear in bed. And something else to wear in the morning. And your head hurts, and the only glimmer of light on the horizon is the possibility of half an hour lying on the sofa during a particularly absorbing edition of 'Sooty'. As a régime, it is not exactly what you might call total bedrest.

So what do you do, if you are not ill enough to precipitate a crisis and bring your husband home from work, or merit a Home Help? The kind of minor illnesses which in your childless days meant a day or two in bed with a comforting hot whisky-and-lemon have turned into a nightmare. Nobody cares about you: if a mother is sufficiently robust to stagger through the day, driven by altruism and necessity, nobody will step in.

Unless you ask. The key lies in asking, and it is no disgrace. I remember one morning when I was alone, being sick for the fourth time in an hour at 8 a.m. with food poisoning, and realizing that the children were starting to get worried. My gay little remarks through the lavatory door – 'Out in a minute – don't worry – has Teddy had his brekky yet?' – were starting to lack conviction. So I staggered out, rang the next-door neighbour and said 'Can't cope. Can you chat to the children while they have breakfast?' and went straight to bed. I was lucky to have the neighbour: no mother should ever allow herself to be on bad terms with the people who live, physically, closest to her. Dear and reliable friends five miles away are not always enough. Apart from neighbours, friends and family and grannies and favourite babysitters will also play their part. With luck. Only ask, shamelessly.

Some young children are capable of real sympathy and help to sick parents. Only, again, you have to explain that you are poorly. I know a single mother who went through a terrible bout of flu, without ever admitting to her son of four that she

felt ill. She didn't want to frighten him. The only result was that the child found her short-tempered and odd and unwilling to hug him, and never knew why. On the third day he burst into tears and said, 'Mummy, don't you love me these days?', and when she said yes, she did, only she felt ill with a bad cold, he was so relieved that he nursed her with dogged enthusiasm and slopped drinks of water all afternoon. Girls, even more, seem to like the idea of a mummy curled on the sofa being looked after, even if you do have to spring to your feet occasionally to avert some disaster. It is definitely worth exhibiting your weakness. A bit.

The only other strategy is to have a little reserve of something exciting, new, and quiet to do in case of illness. I always have had, but I thought originally that it was in case of the children being ill. I kept a box of special easy press-out models to make, transfers, puzzles, new felt-tip colouring pens and so forth. In fact, small poorly children with the brief, acute spells of illness they get do not usually want such things at all. They want good old mangy Mister Rabbit, their revolting old muslin dusters to suck, and to watch a video of Noddy or Paddington, worn thin by endless replaying. It is when *you* are ill that the box of surprises comes into its own. You can lie on the sofa in a light delirious doze, watching them out of the corner of your eye and hoping for better days. After all, now that they have had the virus and your husband has had it and your childminder . . . there can't be anyone left to wreck your life with it. Can there? And there has to be a good gap before the next bug, doesn't there?

Keep taking the vitamins. There's a lot of it about.

21. On the Run: Mummy does a bunk

This is a subversive chapter. It flies in the face of convention and tradition. It does not fit in with the correct, approved patterns of happy family life. If you intend to read it in a public place, you had better carefully Tipp-ex over the title and print in something more acceptable, something a mother ought to be seen reading. Like 'Terry Nappies Can Be Fun!' or 'Help Your Unborn Foetus Get Ahead With Maths!' That way, everyone will think you are a proper, dutiful, perfect wife and mother who would never dream of fleeing the nest in search of adventure. For this is about holidays: short breaks, weekends, or even weeks. But it is not about buckets and spades and theme parks, oh no. Nor is it about those 'working-on-your-marriage', or 'second honeymoon' weekends away *à deux* with your man, while Granny minds the children. They may have their place, but in my observation whenever two parents of young children go away together there is always one of them who keeps phoning home and sniffling, while the other buys up shopfuls of designer dungarees and spaceships out of pure guilt.

Both the above categories come in for broad social approval. Holidays with children – Aaaah! Lovely! Weekends away with husbands – Aaah! Lovely! It's so important to keep marriages fresh, for the sake of the whole family, isn't it? Everyone approves. However, what I am talking about is the unspeakable: holidays for *mothers only*. I am talking about women who quite deliberately, despite the hissing of their neighbours and the raised eyebrows of their own mothers, announce that they are off for a few days all by themselves. The children can stay with Daddy, or Auntie, or Granny, or sleep a few nights at a friend's house, but Mummy is off. That thing in the hall is Mummy's rucksack. Goodbye. See you on Monday.

Before anyone starts to go into a long wailing lament about

157

how rough this is on the children, stop and think. Mothers go off to hospital to have new babies: sometimes they aren't back for over a week. They go off to nurse their old parents, or help their sisters-in-law with babies; and nobody condemns them for that. Everybody recognizes that children – once off the breast – actually cope perfectly well with short separation if the basic relationship is good; and that they recover quickly afterwards from any crossness or nervousness. Nobody cavils at your going off to nurse someone or have another baby (or even to be alone with your husband working-on-your-marriage) because everyone accepts that these are Good Causes. It seems that as long as women with children are somehow sacrificing themselves kindly for others – any others – they escape criticism.

Men generally escape it anyway. There is a well-established feeling that a man needs his hobbies. He needs his time away from the missus and kids. On the whole, society feels that even if he goes off to the office daily, there is actually something healthy about Daddy nipping off for a weekend's sailing with his mates, or going up north for the big match. But as for mothers – no chance. There is still a taboo about sloping off on your own for fun when you should be cutting up cucumbers into the shape of rabbits and listening to small people reading tedious stories about Roger Red-Hat and Mrs Red-Hat and all the other blasted Red-Hats. Never mind that you do these things dutifully for the other three hundred and sixty days of the year: if you skive off on a private holiday you will still feel, and be made to feel, like a selfish bitch. So let us blow this nonsense wide apart and say loud and clear and confidently that private breaks are good for mothers, and therefore good for their families.

After all, we are only human. Beneath that layer of bland, mumsy cheerfulness and oops-a-daisy, reassuring competence, we are the same uncertain, hopeful, adventurous girls we always were. We are not discontented, we are not planning to desert the nest permanently, we are not (perish the thought) looking for lissome young men to conquer. Can't be bothered with lissome young men. It is just that sometimes, for a few days, there is something wonderful about walking away from the lives we have so carefully built up. Goodbye house, goodbye garden, goodbye cooker; goodbye educational toys which keep getting scattered into uneducational heaps of litter, goodbye Peter Rabbit mugs, goodbye telephone and babysitting circle and dinner-money envelopes; goodbye to all the clutter and fuss of everyday living. And because the children are small, and personally cause most of the clutter and fuss, then it has to be goodbye to them, too. For a few days. And goodbye husband: partly because someone has to hold the fort, and he is probably the safest bet; but partly because every married woman needs occasional breaks in order to remember who she used to be before she was Mrs and before she was Mummy.

Where shall she go? Depends on taste, and on money. Since my youngest turned three I have tried three different escapes. The first consisted of setting out two days before the family on our annual holiday to Ireland, taking with me a hiking tent and a rucksack. I spent the nights sleeping on the cold hard ground, all alone on a remote Western island with clouds flying across a full moon. All day I read *The Pilgrim's Progress*, walked, bought goats' milk from the farm and toasted my sausages on tent pegs over a teeny Camping-gaz stove in the rain. I never washed much, but every day I jumped from a flat warm rock into the icy sea, and ran around to dry off in the wind. There were no mirrors. Sometimes I met other campers or hikers and had a desultory chat; but for two days I had no schedule, nobody to satisfy, and was responsible for nobody but myself.

It set me up, I swear it, to be a better Mummy for eighteen months. I remembered things, ways of thinking, paths of freedom which I had forgotten since my hippy teens. I became more like an older sister, for a while, and fussed a lot less about the ghastly mess on the playroom floor. I was readier to join in crazy, messy games, and invent them, and less fixated on getting everyone to bed slap bang on time.

When that wore off I spent a hilarious weekend in Scotland trying to learn cross-country skiing with an old schoolfriend. We slept in a bunkhouse with a lot of rather serious teenagers reading Proust paperbacks, and disgraced ourselves by going out to drink pints of old-and-filthy with the Royal Pioneer Corps cross-country ski team. We were transported to the frosty slopes in a repellent old red van, singing rude songs. We felt sixteen again.

When that was only a golden memory, a year later, I took a whole week and splashed out some savings to ship as paying crew aboard a one hundred-foot Brixham trawler in the Hebrides. The curious thing about that trip was that I got through an average of half a bottle of Scotch every night, in between practising the penny whistle very badly and singing mournfully to a Gaelic harp until one a.m., and still got home clear-eyed and bounding with health. Indeed, after each of these excursions into irresponsible depravity I have returned feeling wonderful, and cheerfully resumed my respectable life of sleeping in a bed, drinking one glass of wine a fortnight and cutting twenty small finger and toe nails by way of a Saturday night treat. I was far nicer to the family than before, and threw fewer tantrums. Next time, I plan to try a long-distance path.

You don't, of course, have to be as hearty in your tastes as that. But I would not recommend lying on a beach, either. If you do, you will think constantly of how much the children would have liked it. Even a health farm could give you too much time for reflection and guilt. The ideal break is one which makes you *do* something, and learn something adult and challenging and irrelevant to the rest of your life. Abseiling, for instance. Or Russian. There are courses which teach you to drive Suffolk Punches, and others which train you in circus skills like juggling, stilt-walking and riding a unicycle. Anyone who can run a couple of under-eights should find all that comes pretty naturally. If you want to be really original, there is a place where you go and they give you a piece of wood and a chisel and a tutor, and by the end of your few days you have carved and painted a fine wooden decoy duck to take home as a talisman. If you have no money at all, you could go and paint a bachelor-girlfriend's flat and go to the pub with her in the evenings.

But you can get plenty of long weekends for the price of two pairs of jeans; seek out a course designed for students, or – if

you're really broke – just take a very long hike or bike ride with
a couple of girlfriends or a stray cousin. You could stay in a
farmhouse for £5 a night, take a sketch pad with you and try
to draw a passable pig. If you want to be sure of pleasant,
unthreatening female company, the WI runs countless residen-
tial courses; if you want to pray, go on a monastic retreat; if
you want to do some good, go and join a gang of railway
restorers, or volunteer canal navvies, or be a Conservation
Corps volunteer and hack through overgrown woodlands. It is
usually students who do all this, but there is no reason a run-
away mummy shouldn't have a go. One old friend of mine
recently abandoned her very demanding family of five under-
eights in a country rectory to spend a long weekend helping
teach young offenders to shoot rapids in canoes. All the professional social workers returned exhausted, but she was radi-
ant with the sheer different-ness of it all.

161

Whatever you do, it will be even better if it makes you mix with other adults, randomly selected. One can become horribly limited by mixing only with other parents of young children, people from your own age and social set who live in your own part of town. A few aspiring unicyclists or ploughmen might make a change. One of the greatest joys of my week on the Brixham trawler was that I had to pull on ropes with teenagers and pensioners, redundant cotton-mill operatives and nurses, the single and the feckless. I remembered, suddenly, that there are other kinds of people in the world than mummies, daddies, uncles, aunties, grannies and teachers.

And let there be no guilt. After all, we come home from these excursions feeling fresh, amused, interested in life, and delighted to see our children again. We marvel, after a few days away, to see how nice they are, how clever and beautiful and original and loving. As the poet said, 'What do they know of England, who only England know?' How can you appreciate the joys of parenthood when you have your nose rubbed in them every day?

22. Is That All There Is? The last baby

Imagine a group of women friends, all in the same neighbourhood. They had their first babies at around the same time, shared coffee and sympathy and hints on teething. Then, one by one, they announced their second pregnancies and produced siblings. A community of children grew up, going to one another's birthday parties and starting playgroup and school together. All very tidy: the classic two-per-family. Everyone had enough room in their car, enough seat belts, enough bunk beds for children to sleep overnight in each other's houses. The mothers gradually got their figures back.

Then, one fateful day, one of the mothers yawned and started refusing coffee and spirits, and kept leaving dinner parties early. 'Well, yes, you might as well know . . . May, actually . . .' Consternation, gossip, envy. Strange broody stirrings ran through the group, and the husbands shifted uneasily, with sidelong glances. Non-pregnant mothers began to look with a new discontent at the way their youngest children were shooting upwards and slimming down, out of nappies and cots forever. They started taking detours past the maternity hospital, gazing up at its windows, thinking what it would be like to go in there again, huge and nervous and excited, and to come out a few days later with a new person in their arms. Those who enjoyed birth and studied it eagerly the first time round felt aggrieved that all that wonderful equipment was still there inside them – eggs, tubes, muscles – but would never be used again, would wither and atrophy into menopausal uselessness. Was that warm cosy womb, nicely run in, with only two previous careful owners, never going to have another tenant? Those breasts, never feed again? And what about the baby clothes, the rattles, the playpen, the buggy . . . shouldn't some decision be made?

The story has alternative endings. Maybe most of the women pulled out of their broody mood, and contented themselves with cuddling the new baby. Perhaps several of them followed down this path, encouraged by her example to carry out their long-cherished, secret plan to have more children. They discovered, if so, that society looks askance on big families today: that four or five children is no longer dubbed a 'fine family', but seen as a sort of perverse self-indulgence. They discovered that people who, before, would gladly ask two adults and two children round to lunch or for the weekend, boggled at the thought of this overwhelming crowd. And they discovered the joys of big families, too: the tribal closeness and the way that there always seems to be someone free to amuse the newest baby.

The point is this: because the twentieth century has given us better control than ever before over our reproductive lives, modern couples have to ask themselves, in a way our grandmothers rarely did, the question 'Have I had my last baby?' It is a surprisingly painful question. Apart from sheer physical broodiness – that yearning for another floppy little downy head and sucky little mouth, for an uncertain, new smile and a joyful pair of waving legs – many of us harbour a deep sense of unease about limiting our families artificially. The unease actually gets worse the more babies you have. For whereas it may be sensible, practical and utterly reasonable to call a halt when your home and your finances and lifestyle demand it, reasonableness is not everything. Once you have had such a close brush with elemental life forces as you do in childbirth, mere common sense loses some of its attraction. We have felt new life kicking inside us, feared for it, protected it, longed for it and finally brought it forth in painful triumph and fed it from our breasts. We have loved it quite unreasonably. Watch any pale mother and father standing over a hopeless scrap of flesh in a hospital incubator, willing it to live on even in disability, and you will admit the glorious unreasonableness of parenthood. Whatever light-hearted jokes we may crack about the maternity ward, however much we claim to hate messy nappies and broken nights, we never quite lose our secret reverence for childbirth.

Nothing so momentous ever happens to us, before or afterwards.

So saying a firm 'No' to another baby is, on one level, quite sensible. On that other level, half-consciously, it feels like an outrage against nature.

There is also a strong streak of Peter Pan in some of us. After all, when we stop being 'young mothers', and let our children grow up and go to school, when we give away the potty and high chair and floral smocks, we are closing a chapter of our own lives. Life with new babies and fast-developing crazy toddlers was an exhausting, exciting journey, sometimes monotonous, sometimes frightening, always wonderful. It is rather like sailing the Atlantic or hacking through an unexplored rain forest. And when any great journey comes to an end, you feel a sense of sadness and loss, and the realization that you have suddenly grown older. Life with growing children is in many ways more demanding, emotionally and intellectually: this entire book has been about those demands, and it has been harder to write, and less full of certainties, than the one I wrote about babyhood. As your children grow up, so must you. The temptation to have a new baby who only wants milk and love and cuddles can sometimes be a longing for escape: not all mothers of big families are like this, but there are some – the Pumpkin Eaters – who actually neglect older children to dote on each new baby. They are like people who are forever starting novels and never get beyond Chapter One. Some women like the excuse of having young babies: as one observed when her youngest reached two, 'This is the crunch. I've either got to have another one or get my figure back.' Some dread the idea of going back to work in a dull office after running a home with brilliant success, yet haven't the confidence to stay at home without the excuse of a small child.

And some feel like the Catholic campaigner against birth control, Mrs Victoria Gillick, who once said something in an interview which I have never been able to forget. Talking of her twelve children (and I have met nine of them, and whatever you think of her, they are a credit to her and Gordon, honestly), she said that having a family was like giving a party. You can

165

either give a well-ordered dinner party with everyone's place laid for them and strict RSVP invitations, or you can just throw the house open, and see who turns up, and make them all welcome and enjoy whatever develops.

Call if feckless if you like, a recipe for poverty and slipshod upbringing; but as a philosophy, it has its own dignity. There is something appealing in the idea of the family as a great, rolling party with the guests sent along by God or fate. If you are one of a big, slap-happy family yourself the appeal is even stronger. At least two of my brothers, so I am assured, were unplanned, but the thought of a world without either of them in it fills me with dismay. What chances missed, what jokes not made, what fiddle tunes not played? What nephews, nieces never born? If I close the options now – surgically, chemically, or however – on having more babies, what marvellous human beings might there be, lurking out there, unborn in nothingness, missing their fated chance?

A load of romantic, broody drivel! you say. What about overpopulation? What about the cost of education? There are a dozen reasons for limiting a family to small numbers, and only a vague philosophical unease and personal taste to stop you. But can you utterly deny that you have ever felt these yearnings yourself? And if you have, did you instantly suppress the feeling, pretend it never happened, and make hearty, efficient, tidy remarks about 'looking forward to having my own life back'? And if you did say that, didn't it give you a hidden, nagging sadness for a while? And don't you now get a bit depressed every time you meet a new baby, smelling of milk and trustfulness, when all you have is a brace of argumentative little politicians?

Of course I'm really glad they're all grown up

If the answer is 'No, I never felt this,' then good luck to you. Your balance is better than most, and better than mine. But if you do suffer from the strange, cosmic sadness that afflicts broody women who – because of circumstance and common sense – have called a halt to reproduction, then why deny it? Don't suffer alone. Don't condemn yourself to brisk, bright lies. Talk about the feeling, revel in it, and if your husband is fearful of financial disaster, try to make him understand that you are not threatening, but mourning something that never can be. We are encouraged to express every weird sexual fantasy, yet shushed when we talk of the longing for another birth: this is absurd. So share the bittersweet mixture of memory and longing, and allow yourself sometimes to wonder what the other baby – the phantom, unconceived baby – might have been like. Even grieve, if you want to. There is nothing weak, or wrong, or unnatural about broodiness – even in a woman with six children already. It is just life trying to get out. You can stop it, but don't deny its force.

The other way out of the dilemma, of course, is to fling caution, cap and pills to the four winds and have another baby. Or two, or three. But that is another story.

23. Envoi: More to them than meets the eye

Mozart was composing fluently at five years old. So was Dolly Parton.

The historian Thomas Macaulay, who could read fluently at three, spent the months running up to his seventh birthday in writing a treatise intended to convert the natives of Malabar to Christianity. It is not recorded whether it worked.

John Stuart Mill spoke Greek before he was four, and wrote a history of Rome at six and a half, but later regretted the childhood he lost.

The average four-year-old knows 1,500 words. By five it is 2,072, rising to 2,562 by the sixth birthday. It is not recorded how many of them are rude.

Louis XIV, the Sun King, succeeded four months before his fifth birthday, and was hailed as the leader (and legally, the physical owner) of nineteen million people. However, shortly after this he nearly drowned in a pond because nobody was bothering to watch him.

Paul Klee, the Swiss painter, drew so vividly at four that he frightened himself into fits. He thought the devils he had drawn were coming to life.

The present Dalai Lama was enthroned at five. The Venerable Bede entered his monastery at seven.

Busby Berkeley was performing professionally at five. So were the acrobat Blondin, and Vesta Tilley, who had hit on her *métier* very early: she was already performing in male drag, complete with a natty little moustache. Shirley Temple got her first Oscar at six. Fred Astaire was touring at seven.

Maréchal Foch of France began studying military history in earnest at six.

Churchill, at seven, was bottom of the class, and considered untalented, dull, and uncooperative. Only the uncooperativeness endured into later life.

Sigmund Freud at the same age once deliberately wee-weed in his parents' bedroom. His father said: 'That boy will never amount to anything.'

And if you must express your anger Sigmund, I'd prefer you not to do it on the carpet —

Henry VI presided over the State Opening of Parliament at three and – according to chroniclers – 'Shryked and cryed and sprang' throughout the ceremony.

Federico Fellini ran off with a circus at seven.

At four years old James VI had eight tutors, and at eight was described as 'a living lexicon' of languages. Prince Albert educated his son Bertie so early and rigorously that when Bertie became Edward VII, he could hardly bear to educate his own sons at all, but shoved them into the Navy.

In Japan, Suzuki violin pupils play Mendelssohn at five.

In Bombay, young children are recruited as effective and skilled public health workers, diagnosing scabies and giving rehydration therapy in Child to Child schemes. It works because, say the organizers, children 'are keen, know their own community, and are not threatening and frightening as doctors can be'.

Saint Francis Xavier said, 'Give me the children until they are seven and anyone may have them afterwards.'

Index

(compiled by author)

Accents (children's) 128ff
Advertising 37, 78ff
Animals 71ff
Arbitration 41–2
Archers, The 128
Art galleries 140

Babysitters 51ff
Bachelor, uncles/aunts 55ff
Birthday cakes 113
Birthday parties 110ff
Birthday teas 113
Books 132
Bottoms, private nature of 104, 106ff
Broodiness 163ff
Bum-talk 105
Burn-out (children's) 46

Casualty wards 147ff
Cats 71, 73
Children (other people's) 110ff
Clothes 66ff
Coaching 45ff
Collectable toys 79
Competition, inter-mother 21–3
Computers 85
Convalescence 152

Death 6, 76–7, 94

Depression (yours) 43
Dignity 43
Discipline 16, 25, 18–21
Doctors 150, 152–3
Dogs 71
Dressing-up 136

Eating 30
Education 118–9
Entertainers 114

Fairness 39ff
Fairs 141
Father Christmas 95, 100ff
Femininity 67
Fears (children's) 101–2
Films 139–40
Fish, pet 75
Friends (children's) 11–16, 126–7
Friends (yours) 18–21, 162

Games, party 112
Gerbils 74–5
Grannies 89ff, 135–6, 138
Guilt (yours) 21, 33, 45, 78, 74, 82
Guinea-pigs 73–4

Holidays 141ff, 157
Hospitals 146ff

Index

Illness 151ff

Justice, dispensing 35, 42–3

Kicking 32

Language 131–2
Legends 99

Marxism 62
Monetarism 62
Money, handling 29, 59ff
Multiculturalism 99
Museums 139–40

Neighbours 104
Nursing 152

Parties 110ff
Party bags 115
Pass the parcel 114
Pets 71ff
Politics 95–6
Ponies 76
Possessions 42–3
Poverty 60ff
Punishment 32–4

Questions (children's) 5, 8, 10

Rabbits 73–4
Reading 124–5

Religion 94ff

Sailing lessons 45
School 14, 112, 116ff
Sexuality 106ff
Sharing 14
Siblings 39ff, 125–6, 163
Slapping 30–3
Sleepovers 53–5
Socialization 7, 51–2
Spending 64
Spitting 32
Spoiling 82
Sport 45ff
Sports day 23
Steam fairs 141
Strangers 55ff
Swearing 29, 107, 129
Swopping 64

Television 5, 35ff, 97, 103
Theatres 136–7
Theme parks 140–1
Three, changes at 5–6
Tooth fairy 95, 100
Toys 78ff
Treats 135ff
Trips 135ff

Videos 36–7

Wealth 61ff
Witches 102–3
Whining 29–30

How *Not* to Be a Perfect Mother

Libby Purves

Perfect Mothers:
smile serenely
run immaculate homes
make nappies into kites
read books on Child Development
never raise their voices

Real Mothers:
have food on their jumpers
never finish anything
limp from treading on Sticklebricks
read romantic novels on the quiet
squeak with exhaustion

With sparkling humour and a low cunning born of four years spent catching food before it hits the floor, Libby Purves shows that even the most unpromising madonna can survive the years of looking after babies and toddlers.

Drawing on her own experience of domestic havoc with two babies, and on the wit and wisdom of fifty like-minded mothers, Libby Purves shamelessly describes how to cut the corners and bend the rules which never mattered much anyway.

An invaluable guide to being an imperfect mother and enjoying it.

One Summer's Grace

A Family Voyage Round Britain

Libby Purves

In the summer of 1988 Libby Purves and her husband Paul Heiney set sail in their cutter *Grace O'Malley* with their children Nicholas, aged five, and Rose, three. They sailed the 1,700 miles around Britain, from the offshore labyrinths of the sandy south-east to the towering stacks of Cape Wrath and back home through the North Sea. Her account of the voyage is a new classic of the sea.

'It is that rarest of all books on the yachting shelf – a work of acerbic realism. Libby Purves is wonderfully sharp on the woes of containing a marriage and a family inside their pressure-cooker of a small boat. Her portrait of coastal Britain in the 1980s is wise, affectionate and sceptical; her pleasure in our scary seas rings true because there is not a word of cant or overstatement in her story. This is how it is – and Miss Purves tells it beautifully'

Jonathan Raban

'A delightful book, warm, wise and candid'　*Sunday Telegraph*

How Not to Be a Perfect Family

Libby Purves

PERFECT FAMILIES

Tidy everything away neatly
Tick off museums in the guidebook
Work hard and play fair
Show respect for one another

REAL FAMILIES

Keep their worldly goods on the stairs and in the kitchen
Start fights in the Louvre
Do their homework on the school bus and cheat at Monopoly
Tie the shoelaces of sleeping Uncles together after Christmas
   dinner

Having cast a witty and realistic eye over the perils of being a perfect mother and raising a perfect child, Libby Purves now turns her hand to 'the cornerstone of life' – the family.

Giving us the benefit of her hard-won wisdom on the subjects of housewives and househusbands, privacy and nudity, television, computer games, sibling rivalry, rules and laying down the law, grandparents and not-so-grandparents, house moves, school troubles, adolescents, crises and crunches, marriage maintenance, and family fun, fights and holidays, Libby Purves emerges with sense of humour intact and an armful of practical hints.

Whether yours is a sanctuary or a madhouse, this level-headed celebration of family life will make you laugh and cringe with recognition. Best of all, it will reassure you that no-one else has a perfect family either!

ISBN 0 00 638121 9

Letters from School

John Rae

'Why doesn't the head do something about it?' is a familiar cry from parents of schoolchildren. Bullying, racism, drugs, sex, corporal punishment – all parents have their own opinions on such issues and how best to deal with them.

In *Letters from School* John Rae has written the letters he wishes he had been able to write as a headmaster. For sixteen years, and with great energy and success, he ran Westminster School, among the oldest and most famous of English public schools; his often controversial views attracted considerable attention in the education world and in the media. Now, for the first time, he has written freely about his job. His letters use imaginary people and situations, but the issues are real, based entirely on his own experience.

They provide unique insight into a job that tests the nerve and stamina more than most.

'Once I had started to read I could not stop until I got to the end.'
Mary Warnock

The Family Welcome Guide 1994

Malcolm Hamer and Jill Foster

The Family Welcome Guide is the only comprehensive and authoritative guide to the best hotels, self-catering accommodation, pubs, restaurants and places to visit for parents and children.

Over 600 establishments are listed, with maps to help you locate them. Every one extends a friendly welcome to all the family, and provides the essential basic services: hotels with cots, high chairs, a free baby-listening service; pubs with separate family rooms; and restaurants with high chairs and special menus for children. If you are planning some sightseeing, this guide will help you pick the museums, stately homes, wildlife and theme parks with the best facilities for families.

Whether you are planning a meal or day out, a journey or a holiday, don't leave home without it!

'The entries in the guide are informative, practical and bear the stamp of honest, down-to-earth assessment.'   *Observer*

'An essential handbook for anyone planning a family outing.'
Parents Magazine

ISBN 0 00 638112 X

Hollywood vs. America
Popular Culture and the War on Traditional Values

Michael Medved

This book has struck a raw nerve. Film stars, commentators and politicians joined the fierce debate fuelled by Michael Medved's trenchant critique of the film industry – the most provocative study of the moral implications of popular culture ever written. His condemnation of sex, violence, bad language, and the seemingly consistent attack on traditional values, has given rise to feverish discussions on both sides of the Atlantic. Jane Fonda has accused Hollywood of immortality. Sir Anthony Hopkins may not now recreate the monstrous role of Hannibal Lecter.

Why do so many films attack religion, glorify violence and undermine the family? What is the cost of big-screen brutality? Have we become impervious to the increasingly grotesque violence erupting from our cinema screens and high-street video shops?

Greeted both with cheers of support and howls of enraged dissent, *Hollywood vs. America* confronts head on one of the most significant issues of our time.

'Real dynamite . . . The author says his book will make him the most hated man in Hollywood. On the other hand, it might save an industry that seems bent on self-destruction.'   *Daily Mail*

ISBN 0 00 638235 5

All these books are available from your local bookseller or can be ordered direct from the publishers.

To order direct just list the titles you want and fill in the form below:

Name: _____

Address: _____

_____

Postcode: _____

Send to: HarperCollins Mail Order, Dept 8, HarperCollins *Publishers*, Westerhill Road, Bishopbriggs, Glasgow G64 2QT.

Please enclose a cheque or postal order or your authority to debit your Visa/Access account –

Credit card no: _____

Expiry date: _____

Signature: _____

– to the value of the cover price plus:

UK & BFPO: Add £1.00 for the first and 25p for each additional book ordered.

Overseas orders including Eire, please add £2.95 service charge.

Books will be sent by surface mail but quotes for airmail despatches will be given on request.

24 HOUR TELEPHONE ORDERING SERVICE FOR ACCESS/VISA CARDHOLDERS –

TEL: GLASGOW 041-772 2281 or LONDON 081-307 4052